Instructor's Manual

for

Legal Research and Writing for Paralegals

Fourth Edition

by

Deborah E. Bouchoux

ASPEN
PUBLISHERS

111 Eighth Avenue, New York, NY 10011
www.aspenpublishers.com

© 2005 Deborah E. Bouchoux

All rights reserved
Printed in the United States of America

ISBN 0-7355-5106-5

This manual is made available as a courtesy to law teachers with the understanding that it will not be reproduced, quoted or cited, except as where indicated. In the event that anyone would like to cite the manual for thoughts drawn from it, a reference to the relevant page number of the materials text (with the formula "suggested by") may be appropriate.

Copies of this manual are available on computer diskette. Teachers who have adopted the casebook may obtain a copy of the diskette, free of charge, by calling the Aspen Publishers sales assistant at 1-800-950-5259.

Permissions
Aspen Publishers
111 Eighth Avenue
New York, NY 10011

1 2 3 4 5

PREFACE

This Instructor's Manual is designed to accompany the text *Legal Research and Writing for Paralegals* (4th ed. 2005). While the text provides valuable information and background material, the heart of any legal research and writing course is the written assignments and projects.

The text and assignments are arranged sequentially so students are able to recognize progress. The text is organized so confidence is gained through a step-by-step approach to mastering the tasks of legal research and writing. The suggestions given in this Manual are just that – suggestions. You may find that other techniques and strategies work better for you and your students than those provided here. You should feel free to modify assignments and other materials to suit your needs.

This Manual will provide a general review of the text, sample syllabi and overview of individual class sessions, a brief discussion of the students in paralegal programs, teaching strategies, suggestions regarding using the law library, detailed discussions of each chapter in the text, assignments and answer keys (for the end-of-chapter exercises and "State Your Answer" exercises), and a concise Test Bank.

There have been significant changes in access to legal sources since the publication of the third edition of the text. Obtaining statutes, cases, articles on legal topics, and other law-related materials has been greatly enhanced through use of the Internet. Therefore, a section at the end of each chapter, entitled "State Your Answer," offers additional questions relating to the materials discussed in each chapter. These questions require students to access relevant Internet sites and locate the type of information an employer will require them to retrieve, such as the name of a state's secretary of state, local court rules, and so forth. Because of the great number of paralegals are employed in California, Florida, New York, and Texas, the Answer Keys for "State Your Answer" provide state-specific answers for these states. Instructors in other states can readily obtain the answers by accessing the Internet sites as directed.

I welcome your comments and input. Please feel free to contact me at the following address:

Deborah E. Bouchoux
Georgetown University
Paralegal Studies Program
1437 37th Street, N.W.
Poulton Hall – Second Floor
Washington, D.C. 20057-1007

NOTE ON ASSIGNMENTS

The Assignments in this Instructor's Manual (both the end-of-chapter Assignments and the State Your Answer Assignments) are duplicates of those in the textbook itself; however, they have been formatted so that instructors can photocopy them directly from this Manual and give them to students who will then fill in their answers directly onto the assignment sheet itself. Answer Keys are provided that are formatted in the same manner, allowing instructors to more readily grade the assignments.

As noted above, specific answers are given to the "State Your Answers" for the following jurisdictions: California, Florida, New York, and Texas. Instructors in other states can readily obtain the correct answers by accessing the Internet sites as directed.

TABLE OF CONTENTS

Textbook Overview 1

Course Outlines, Sample Syllabi, and Class Sessions 7

Teaching Strategies 18

Things I Wish I Knew When I Started Teaching 24

Useful Web Sites for Teachers 31

The Law Library 32

Suggestions for Assignments 35

    Introduction 35

    Uniform Format of Assignments 36

    State Specific Assignments 37

    Timeliness of Assignments 38

    Grading Assignments 40

    Citation Form for Assignments 42

    Book Crunches 42

    Miscellaneous 44

        Conferences 44

        Drafts 44

        Extra Credit 45

        Mini-Memo 45

        Page Limits 46

        Final Projects 46

Chapter by Chapter Resource Information 47

Assignments and "State Your Answers" for all Chapters....................................112

Answer Keys for Assignments and "State Your Answers" for all Chapters 191

Test Bank 301

    Test Questions for Chapters One and Two......................................302

    Test Questions for Chapters Three Through Twelve 306

    Test Questions for Chapters Fifteen Through Nineteen 315

TEXTBOOK OVERVIEW

Chapters One and Two: Finding the Law; The Federal and State Court Systems

Chapters One and Two are designed to provide general background information and material to students. These first class sessions will be predominantly lecture-oriented as students "settle in" and become familiar with each other, their paralegal program, and you. While assignments are provided, these are designed primarily to ensure students visit a law library and build their confidence. Once students realize that the law library can be used similarly to other libraries and that assignments can be mastered, they will be sufficiently confident to move on to increasingly difficult tasks.

Chapter Three: Statutory Law

Chapter Three is organized into two parts. The introductory section on the process of enacting laws is designed for the purpose of building confidence. Once students have achieved a comfort level provided by several class sessions and at least two straightforward library exercises, they will be ready for their first true "open-ended" assignment, requiring them to use the appropriate sources to locate statutes.

The discussion on statutes precedes the chapters relating to case law because locating statutes is generally easier than locating cases. There are fewer sets of books to learn about and use than for cases, for which students must learn about official and unofficial publication of cases, elements of cases, briefing cases, and locating cases through annotated codes, the difficult-to-use digests, and A.L.R. Moreover, the indexes used for finding statutes in U.S.C.A. and U.S.C.S. (and for most state statutes) are very "forgiving." Once students have learned that using an index to locate a statute is similar to using an index in an encyclopedia to locate general information, they will be ready to progress to the more complex subject of case law.

Chapter Four: Case Law and Judicial Opinions

Chapter Four introduces students to the process by which cases are published, what the cases will look like in the case reports, and how to analyze a case by briefing it. The first assignment in Chapter Four is designed to ensure students can identify the elements of a published case. The second assignment requires students to read and analyze a case by briefing it.

Chapter Five: The Use of Digests, Annotated Law Reports, and
Words and Phrases

Once students have gained background information about case law in Chapter Four and have become comfortable with what cases look like and how to read them, they will be ready for the more challenging task of locating cases through digests and A.L.R. and using West's *Words and Phrases* to locate cases interpreting various legal terms.

Chapters Six and Seven: Encyclopedias, Periodicals, Treatises, and Restatements; Miscellaneous Secondary Authorities

Chapters Six and Seven focus on the secondary sources, from the easy-to-use encyclopedias to the more complex treatises to the less commonly used sources such as opinions of attorneys general and jury instructions. Because students' skills at using law books will be sharpened by the previous assignments, they should experience little difficulty in locating and using most secondary sources.

Chapters Eight and Nine: Legal Citation Form; Updating and Validating Your Research

Once students have been introduced to all of the primary and secondary sources, they can progress to the exacting tasks of citation form and case updating and validating. Because they will have examined and used almost all of the major sets of books in the law library, they will have a frame of reference for learning the citation form for these various sources. Consider whether from this point on, students should be expected to use correct *Bluebook* or *ALWD* citation form in all assignments.

Chapter Ten: **Special Research Issues**

Chapter Ten provides a general overview of the less frequently encountered research tasks, such as those involving legislative history, administrative law, and international law. A quick introduction to these areas of law, together with brief assignments for each topic, should be sufficient to familiarize students with the subject matter as well as the books used in each of these fields.

Chapter Eleven: The Digital Library: LEXIS, Westlaw, and Non-Print Research Sources

The primary focus of Chapter Eleven is on computer-assisted legal research. Students will be much more efficient at using LEXIS and Westlaw once they are completely familiar with conventional research sources. Formulating queries for searching on LEXIS and Westlaw (if they use Boolean connectors rather than natural language techniques) is simplified because students have already been mentally formulating queries and using descriptive words and phrases to access other books in the law library.

Chapter Twelve: E-Research: Legal Research Using the Internet

Chapter Twelve (E-Research) provides information on using the Internet for legal research. A glossary of terms and useful Web sites are provided. While some students may need to be coaxed to abandon the security of bound books for the unknown world of the Internet, others may view conventional print research sources as outmoded and be tempted to rely on the Internet for nearly all legal research tasks. Students should become familiar with the advantages and disadvantages of each method of legal research so that clients' needs are served most efficiently and economically. The written assignment is designed to increase confidence and skill in using the Internet to obtain law-related information.

Chapter Thirteen: Overview of the Research Process

Chapter Thirteen provides a review of the research process, together with some tips for getting started on research tasks, taking notes, and working efficiently in a law library. Some students may have become dependent on the question-answer format of the written assignments and may need to become prepared for the "floundering" feeling many beginning researchers experience when presented with open-ended research and writing projects. The worksheet and charts provided in this chapter are intended to reduce the anxiety some beginning researchers experience and should provide an ordered framework for performing complex research tasks.

Chapters Fourteen and Fifteen: Back to Basics; Strategies
for Effective Writing

Because many students do not have strong writing backgrounds, a review of writing basics is usually helpful. Even those students who have done a great deal of writing are unfamiliar with *legal* writing and will benefit from an explanation of the features of effective legal writing. Assignments in these chapters focus on recognizing and correcting common writing errors.

Chapters Sixteen, Seventeen, and Eighteen:
Legal Correspondence; Legal Memoranda; Legal Briefs

Once students have been introduced to the hallmarks of effective legal writing and have reviewed the basics of grammar, spelling, and punctuation, they will be ready to tackle writing projects. The chapters on writing describe the most common writings performed by many legal professionals: correspondence, internal office memoranda, and briefs for trial and appellate courts. Each of these projects requires an interplay of the research skills learned in the earlier chapters and writing skills learned in the later chapters. Each project uses a different style and tone so that at the completion of these projects, students should be prepared for the writing tasks that await them in the "real world."

Chapter Nineteen: Postwriting Steps

Chapter Nineteen focuses on the finishing touches for writing projects: reviewing, revising, editing, and proofreading. Careful proofreading skills are essential for paralegals due to the exacting nature of the legal profession.

SUMMARY

Each chapter in the text is designed to build upon previously introduced information, with the earlier chapters concentrating on providing background information and building confidence, the middle chapters focusing on developing the skills needed for any type of research project, and the later chapters devoted to the task of linking research skills to writing skills. This step-by-step approach will allow students to progress in an orderly manner enabling them to become confident and efficient researchers and effective writers.

COURSE OUTLINES, SAMPLE SYLLABI, AND CLASS SESSIONS

COURSE OUTLINES/SYLLABI

Legal research programs and classes vary greatly from institution to institution. Some classes meet once per week for two or three hours. Others meet twice or more each week for an hour or slightly longer.

On the following pages, I have provided suggested course outlines/syllabi, including text assignments for *Legal Research and Writing for Paralegals* (4th ed. 2005), for two different course formats: a one and one-half hour class session and a three-hour class session. You may find that some other schedule better suits your needs and those of your students.

After more than 20 years of teaching legal research and writing to students, I have found that students like having a definite course syllabus and that while they are willing to be flexible to some extent, they are more comfortable when a syllabus lends predictability to class sessions.

I have also found that, as is the case with almost everything else in the law, it is better to put things in writing. Therefore, my syllabus usually consists of two sections. The first section is devoted to some of the goals and rules for the class, the grading policy, required texts, and a telephone number where I can be reached. Including your (or your institution's) policy on attendance, grading, late assignments, or any other similarly sensitive issue will serve as a reminder to students who have selective memories regarding these matters. The second section of the syllabus includes the schedule of the class, due dates for assignments and projects, and reading assignments. Once again, including the dates assignments are due eliminates any confusion on this topic.

Some instructors prefer to allocate a portion of the student's final grade to class participation and attendance. Such a policy (especially when students are called upon at random) helps ensure that students complete all assignments and are ready for class. Other instructors do not include participation as a component of grades (believing that such a policy encourages some students to "hog" the floor while penalizing shy students), while still others reserve the right to include participation in borderline cases.

State in your syllabus if you have any requirements as to format of assignments, such as requiring typed or computer-generated assignments in 12-point font.

While many legal research and writing instructors assign grades solely on the basis of research and writing exercises and projects, others prefer to give exams as well to test students' knowledge of the material. Clearly, either approach is acceptable. One slight disadvantage of giving tests is that tests will "use up" class time that many instructors prefer to devote to introducing material, discussing writing tips and strategies, and reviewing assignments completed by students. A concise Test Bank is found at the end of this Manual.

Because you will surely be asked if "extra credit" assignments are available, consider your policy on this and include it in the syllabus.

Due to the significant amount of material in paralegal classes, I have often had to omit some topics from class discussions and tests and simply suggest that students review those materials on their own. It can be difficult to cover all of the topics in the text in the number of hours allotted for the class in some paralegal programs. Thus, you may wish to focus on those areas that you believe will be of greatest value to paralegals in the workplace.

A number of paralegal programs and instructors now post their syllabi on various websites. Using a general search engine (for example, www.google.com), key in the terms "paralegal syllabus" or similar terms and you will be directed to numerous syllabi that you can review for suggestions.

The following website offers valuable information on preparing a syllabus for a course, what to include in the syllabus, and samples of course syllabi: http://www.honolulu.hawaii.edu/intranet/committees/FacDevCom/guidebk/teachtip/teachtip.htm#syllabus.

Following are sites providing some specific syllabi for legal research and writing courses:

- http://www.uwf.edu/justice/spring2005/tatumpla4155.doc
- http://www.wscc.cc.tn.us/businessdiv/legal/syllabilaw1200.asp
- http://faculty.dbcc.cc.fl.us/cupick/pla1103.html
- http://www.hccs.edu/discipline/POFT/pofl2305.html
- http://academic.pg.cc.md.us/~trhodes/legal%20research%20syllabus.htm
- http://www.donovanlegalstudies.com/legsyl.f01.pdf
- www.aafpe.org (AAfPE offers sample syllabi. Your institution is likely a member of AAfPE and thus can provide you with access to the syllabi AAfPE provides.)

Other sample syllabi can be found at http://jurist.law.pitt.edu/cour_pgs.htm. This site, designed especially for those engaged in the teaching of law, provides a wealth of valuable information for law teachers, including sample course outlines, syllabi, and exam collections.

SAMPLE SYLLABUS

FOR

LEGAL RESEARCH AND WRITING

(One and One-Half Hour Class Sessions)

GEORGETOWN UNIVERSITY
PARALEGAL STUDIES PROGRAM
LEGAL RESEARCH AND WRITING
FALL 2005

Class Time:	8:00 a.m. – 9:30 a.m.
Instructor:	Deborah E. Bouchoux (xxx) xxx-xxxx E-mail: xxxxxxxxxxx
Texts:	*Legal Research and Writing for Paralegals* (4th ed. 2005) by Deborah E. Bouchoux The *Bluebook* (18th ed. 2005)
Course Description:	The purpose of this course is to acquaint students with the fundamentals of legal research and writing. Students will learn to use and locate primary and secondary authorities. The course will include a general overview of the federal and state court systems. Students will learn the elements of a court decision, how to locate cases through the use of digests, and how to brief a case. The course reviews the techniques of legal writing customarily taught in law school; citation form; cite checking; the methods of compiling legislative histories; administrative and international legal research; and the writing of letters, law office memoranda, and court briefs.
Assignments:	There are no tests in this class. Grades are based solely on projects assigned and completed. Any assignment that is not turned in promptly at the beginning of a class is late. It will automatically be penalized five points (ten points for the final project) and will thereafter be penalized one point for each day (or fraction thereof). **NO EXCEPTIONS ARE MADE OR GIVEN TO THIS POLICY.** All assignments were prepared at the Georgetown Law Center Law Library. You many find many other sources in other

libraries; however, it cannot be assured or guaranteed that you can complete assignments elsewhere.

Grading: There are 500 points possible. The library assignments (end of chapter exercises and "State Your Answer" exercises) total 200 points. The letter is worth 100 points and the court brief is worth 200 points. The total number of points you achieve will be divided by five and your grade will be assigned as follows (Georgetown University Grading Guidelines):

95 - 100	A
93 - 94	A-
88 - 92	B+
85 - 87	B
82 - 84	B-
80 - 81	C+
78 - 79	C
75 - 77	C-
71 - 74	D+
65 - 70	D
0 - 64	F

LEGAL RESEARCH AND WRITING

SYLLABUS

DATE	TOPIC	ASSIGNMENT
Session 1	Introduction to Legal Systems; Sources of Law	Text: Chapter 1
Session 2	The Federal Court System	Chapter 2; **Ch. 1 Assignments due**
Session 3	Introduction to Statutory Law	Chapter 3; **Ch. 2 Assignments due**
Session 4	Statutory Law and Constitutions; Research Process	
Session 5	Introduction to Judicial Opinions	Chapter 4; **Ch. 3 Assignments due**
Session 6	Judicial Opinions, continued	
Session 7	How to Brief a Case	**Ch. 4 Assignments due**
Session 8	Digests	Chapter 5; **Case brief due**
Session 9	Annotated Law Reports and *Words and Phrases*	
Session 10	Secondary Sources (encyclopedias and periodicals)	Chapter 6; **Ch. 5 Assignments due**
Session 11	Secondary Sources (treatises, restatements, etc.)	
Session 12	Misc. Secondary Sources	Chapter 7; **Ch. 6 Assignments due**
Session 13	Citation Form and Case Updating	Chapters 8 and 9 **Ch. 7 Assignments due**
Session 14	Legislative History; Administrative Law; and International Law	Chapter 10 **Ch. 8 & 9 Assignments due**

Session 15	The Digital Library	Chapters 11 and 12; **Ch. 10 Assignments due**
Session 16	Legal Writing	Chapters 13, 14 and 15; **Ch. 11 & 12 Assignments due**
Session 17	Correspondence and Memoranda	Chapters 16 and 17
Session 18	Brief Writing and Post-Writing	Chapters 18 and 19; **Letter due**
Session 19	Final Session	**Brief due**; in class proofreading assignment

SAMPLE SYLLABUS

FOR

LEGAL RESEARCH AND WRITING

(Three Hour Class Sessions)

**GEORGETOWN UNIVERSITY
PARALEGAL STUDIES PROGRAM
LEGAL RESEARCH AND WRITING
FALL 2005**

Class Time:	8:00 a.m. – 11:00 a.m.
Instructor:	Deborah E. Bouchoux (xxx) xxx-xxxx E-mail: xxxxxxxxx
Texts:	*Legal Research and Writing for Paralegals* (4th ed. 2005) by Deborah E. Bouchoux The *Bluebook* (18th ed. 2005)
Course Description:	The purpose of this course is to acquaint students with the fundamentals of legal research and writing. Students will learn to use and locate primary and secondary authorities. The course will include a general overview of the federal and state court systems. Students will learn the elements of a court decision, how to locate cases through the use of digests, and how to brief a case. The course reviews the techniques of legal writing customarily taught in law school; citation form; cite checking; the methods of compiling legislative histories; administrative and international legal research; and the writing of letters, law office memoranda, and court briefs.
Assignments:	There are no tests in this class. Grades are based solely on projects assigned and completed. Any assignment that is not turned in promptly at the beginning of a class is late. It will automatically be penalized five points (ten points for the final project) and will thereafter be penalized one point for each day (or fraction thereof). **NO EXCEPTIONS ARE MADE OR GIVEN TO THIS POLICY.** All assignments were prepared at the Georgetown Law Center Law Library. You many find many other sources in other

libraries; however, it cannot be assured or guaranteed that you can complete assignments elsewhere.

Grading: There are 500 points possible. The library assignments (end of chapter exercises and "State Your Answer" exercises) total 200 points. The letter is worth 100 points and the court brief is worth 200 points. The total number of points you achieve will be divided by five and your grade will be assigned as follows (Georgetown University Grading Guidelines):

95 - 100	A
93 - 94	A-
88 - 92	B+
85 - 87	B
82 - 84	B-
80 - 81	C+
78 - 79	C
75 - 77	C-
71 - 74	D+
65 - 70	D
0 - 64	F

LEGAL RESEARCH AND WRITING

SYLLABUS

DATE	TOPIC	ASSIGNMENT
Session 1	Introduction to Legal Systems; Sources of Law; the Federal Court System	Chapters 1 and 2
Session 2	Statutory Law and Constitutions	Chapter 3; **Ch. 1 & 2 Assignments due**
Session 3	Judicial Opinions	Chapter 4; **Ch. 3 Assignments due**
Session 4	How to Brief a Case; Digests; Annotated Law Reports; *Words and Phrases*	Chapter 5; **Ch. 4 Assignments due**
Session 5	Secondary Sources	Chapters 6 and 7; **Ch. 5 Assignments due; Case brief due**
Session 6	Citation Form and Case Updating	Chapters 8 and 9; **Ch. 6 & 7 Assignments due**
Session 7	Special Research Topics (Legislative History, Administrative Law, and International Law); New Technology in Legal Research	Chapters 10, 11, and 12 **Ch. 8 & 9 Assignments due**
Session 8	Introduction to Writing; Writing Basics; Legal Correspondence and Memoranda	Chapters 13, 14, and 15; **Ch. 10, 11, & 12 Assignments due**
Session 9	Brief Writing and Post Writing Steps	Chapters 16 – 19; **Letter due**
Session 10	Final Session	**Brief due**

TEACHING STRATEGIES

Adult Learners

Teaching adult learners is an exciting and satisfying profession. The students who attend paralegal programs are typically enthusiastic about acquiring new skills and are eager to learn. The varied backgrounds of students stimulate classroom participation. Some students may be newly minted graduates. Others may be legal secretaries or otherwise employed by law firms or legal employers and desire to learn more about the law. Some of these students may be attending a paralegal program to obtain a promotion. Others attend as a prelude to law school or with the thought that if they enjoy the work and the profession, they may ultimately attend law school. Still others are mid-career or making career changes. Finally, many students are older or post-retirement or are entering the work force for the first time in a number of years.

I have taught classes in which there has been a gap of more than 40 years between the youngest student and the oldest student. One of the most satisfying results of teaching such classes is to observe the friendships, rapport, and collegiality that develop among students with such diverse backgrounds.

On the other hand, it is extremely challenging for an instructor to meet the needs of students who are sometimes two generations apart and have such differing goals. While all (or nearly all) students in law school share a common goal, namely, to become lawyers, the same cannot be said of all paralegal students. Most intend to become paralegals, but some simply desire to know a bit about the law without investing the significant amounts of time and money law school requires. Others may be functioning as paralegals and simply desire to sharpen their skills while others fully intend to attend law school as soon as possible.

Each of these students brings certain strengths to the classroom. The younger students are often confident and are familiar with being in school. Those who are working or have worked in legal settings often have a wealth of information about "real life" in a law firm or legal department. While older students who have not been in a school setting for a number of years often lack confidence and have concerns they will not be able to keep up with the younger students, they may bring invaluable life experience to the classroom. Often their writing skills are superior to those of younger students and they are usually diligent, eager, and conscientious learners.

In general, adult learners are active learners. They prefer being actively involved in the learning process rather than taking copious notes, reading a textbook, and then being tested on the material. This preference for active learning makes legal research and writing a fun and exciting class.

Because the best way to learn legal research is to do it, students will spend a great deal of time in the law library examining the books and acquiring skill and proficiency at research. The challenging task of using the law books and finding the answers to questions on an assignment is often a welcome change from the passive learning in other classes.

The most satisfying aspect of teaching legal research and writing is to observe the progress made by the students. Instructors who teach other courses often have no way of knowing if students have truly mastered the material or if they have simply learned to be skillful students and test-takers. Legal research and writing instructors are able to observe students gain skill and mastery as they progress from the first class, not knowing the difference between a case and a statute, to the last class, capable of locating primary and secondary authorities and then using those authorities to prepare a clear and cogent written project.

Effective Strategies

For a short period of time in the early 1990s, I had the opportunity to serve as Acting Program Director of the Legal Assistant Program at Georgetown University in Washington, D.C. In the course of my duties, I was able to observe other instructors, meet with students, and review students' written evaluations of their instructors. I was thus able to learn from students their perspective as to which teaching techniques were effective and what students believed hindered their progress. After reviewing numerous evaluations and conferring with students I was able to draw some conclusions relating to three critical aspects of teaching: effective teaching strategies; techniques to establish rapport and maintain control in the classroom; and common complaints about instructors.

Effective Instructors of Adults:

1. Are excited and enthusiastic about their subject and are eager to impart information to their students;

2. Clearly outline course objectives;

3. Give all assignments in writing;

4. Have well-organized class outlines, handouts, and other materials to reduce copious note-taking;

5. Give substantive presentations every class;

6. Do not waste class time getting organized;

7. Expect that adult learners have intellectual capabilities equal to their own and treat them accordingly;

8. Support students' efforts and are patient in helping students who have different educational backgrounds or experiences;

9. Are familiar with required texts, handouts, and other materials;

10. Give realistic assignments and projects using examples that approximate real-life situations;

11. Respond to students' need to know how they are doing in class by promptly returning graded papers with comments so students can improve their work;

12. Handle controversial issues and difficult students firmly and fairly;

13. Know "inside" information about their field and are able to share journals, articles, and other news about the field and employment opportunities;

14. Are quick to learn students' names;

15. Meet their commitments to the class and expect the class to honor deadlines; and

16. Are eager to involve participants and use a variety of teaching techniques in class.

Strategies to Establish Rapport and Maintain Control

1. At the first class session, welcome students, announce the course title, introduce yourself, and give a little background about yourself and the class.

2. At the first class session, briefly review course objectives, distribute the course outline, discuss and perhaps briefly review the texts required for the class, and make announcements that include information such as scheduled class breaks and location of restrooms, telephones, and vending machines.

3. For all classes, start on time. This sets the tone for the following sessions and discourages latecomers.

4. Learn students' names quickly and use them. Using first names establishes an atmosphere of joint learning.

5. Use "we" rather than "I" to remind students that learning is a collaborative effort.

6. Gain the respect and friendship of the class. Occasional hecklers or complainers will find no support for their conduct.

7. Respond to questions openly and directly. If you do not know the answer to a question, offer to find the information, and then do so.

8. Avoid criticism or remarks about the facilities, the administration, or other instructors.

9. Look directly at students. Establish eye contact.

10. Watch for signs of fatigue or restlessness and then change the pace of your delivery, move about the room, allow a break, or introduce audio-visual materials or a new topic.

11. Allow time for questions.

12. Avoid rapid-fire delivery. Repeat material if necessary.

13. Make assignments clear. Major projects should be given in writing as handouts.

14. Try to make your delivery interesting, well organized, and stimulating. Avoid reading from the text or other written materials.

15. Avoid excessive "war stories."

Common Complaints about Instructors

1. Instructor is late or disorganized.

2. Instructor is unprepared for class.

3. Instructor rushes through the material without allowing time for comments, discussion, or questions.

4. Instructor fails to follow course syllabus and makes frequent changes in the class schedule, exams, or projects.

5. Instructor gives unreasonable assignments.

6. Instructor ignores questions or becomes defensive when questions are asked.

7. Instructor is unavailable for discussion or assistance.

8. Instructor does not explain the basis of grades.

9. Instructor is unfamiliar with current topics in the field or relevant journals.

Things I Wish I Knew When I Started Teaching

Following is a brief overview of some rather sensitive topics and the manner in which either I or other instructors I know handle these issues. The suggestions given are mere suggestions and may not be applicable to your situation.

1. **I wish I knew students would arrive late for class**. Some students habitually arrive late for class. In Washington, D.C. with its cold winter climate, late arrivals disrupt the class by having to remove their coats and gloves, organize their umbrellas, and then "set up" for class. Some of my classes are at night and the late arrivals often arrive with dinner, unwrapping their meals, crinkling napkins, and spilling drinks. To discourage late arrivals, consider the following:

    a. Institute a point penalty so that any assignment not turned in promptly at the beginning of a class is marked late. Explain that courts reject late filings and that students need to learn the "rules of the road" as soon as possible. These point penalties encourage promptness.

    b. Remain silent until the student is completely seated. The silence in the classroom is deafening and most students make the effort to appear on time thereafter. This "silent treatment" also works well when students talk during your presentation. When I observe such talking (more than a mere comment or two), I usually stop talking completely for however long it takes for the talkers to realize the room is silent. Once I have their attention, I will continue the presentation. On occasion, I have said, "Excuse me. Are there questions? If not, I will continue."

c. Post a sign on the door indicating that students should wait until the next break to enter the room so as not to disrupt other students.

2. **<u>I wish I knew that students would ask for numerous letters of recommendation</u>**. During my first couple of semesters of teaching, I was inundated with requests for letters of recommendation (nearly all of which were for law school applications). What made the task more difficult is that some students who requested recommendations were only average students. This situation is a bit easier now that most students applying to law school send one complete "packet," including recommendations, to the LSAC central admission center, which then sends separate applications to each school.

To make the task of recommendation-writing somewhat more manageable, consider the following:

a. State that students must earn a grade of "A" or "B" in your class for you to write a letter of recommendation.

b. Require that you be given at least three weeks advance notice for writing a recommendation.

c. Require that students provide you with all materials, stamps, envelopes, etc., copies of their transcripts, and so forth. On some occasions, a former student may ask for a letter of recommendation several years after a class has ended. If you teach several classes, it may be difficult for you to recall the student's performance. Thus, asking for a copy of the student's transcript will jog your memory.

d. Limit the number of letters you will write for any one student. One instructor I know allows only two recommendations per student.

Consider whether you will give a standard "to whom it may concern" letter of recommendation. Students may keep these for years and continue passing out and using your letter for a variety of purposes. Many instructors prefer that they be personally called by a prospective employer and will then write a specific and targeted letter to that employer for its use only.

3. **I wish I knew some students would ask questions primarily to be noticed in class**. If you are confronted with a student who asks so many questions that necessary material is not being covered, consider the following:

   a. Announce that you intend to discuss new material first and that once you are through with your presentation, you will entertain questions.

   b. Note that the student has raised his or her hand and comment that you will respond to questions later.

   c. Comment that you will be happy to answer the question outside of the class session (especially if it is not relevant to the material you presented).

   d. Ask students to write down any questions not covered in that class session and state that you will respond to those questions at the beginning of the next class session.

4. **I wish I knew some students were so eager to get a good grade that they would argue with me over every assignment/grade**. This sensitive issue has been one of the most difficult for me to resolve. Generally, I try to make several comments on papers I grade so that students know what I thought was good about

their papers and what I thought needed improving. In many instances, I have invited students to submit a written argument to me, much as they would a court, with supporting "evidence" to support their position. If students can show me that a case or statute or other authority supports their position, I am happy to "restore" points to them. If I make a mistake (and I have, both in grading papers and in calculating grades), I try to apologize promptly and correct the error. In some classes, I have given a short heart-to-heart talk about the value of learning the material and commented that while I understand that everyone wants to perform well and get a good grade, the important thing is to learn the material and that if students believe they have mastered the material and can find and write about cases, statutes, and so forth, then they will have accomplished their goals.

5. **I wish I knew some students would collaborate unfairly with others when doing assignments.** This is another sensitive issue. In the first class session, I try to note that while brainstorming is a useful technique and that while I expect that students may well share information as to where to find materials in the law library, that when it comes time to "put pen to paper," the product must be that of the student and not the result of collaboration. Many law schools ask students to sign statements either at the beginning of each semester or for each project that work produced is their own. If I notice that students' papers are identical or too similar, I make a comment on the papers and remind the students that work must be their own. If another incident occurs, I submit the papers to my program office and ask for guidance.

6. **I wish I knew some students would occasionally be hostile.** I recently had a student who seemed born to complain. He complained about the classroom, the air conditioning, the assignments, the quality of the printer I used for the written assignments, and nearly everything else. From past experience, I knew that confronting him directly in class (in front of other students) would only make him more hostile. I asked him privately why he was so unhappy and asked if I could do anything. I also requested that he not take up class time with negative comments and to make an appointment with the administration to discuss these problems. He improved slightly but in general remained a negative person in the classroom. These disruptive or hostile students are among the most difficult problems for a teacher and can make one dread going into the classroom. Try killing them with kindness. Try speaking to them privately. Try enlisting the administration for help. Chances are, these students are negative in other classes as well. Perhaps the program director can speak with the student and comment that several instructors have noticed the student's attitude and ask if the program can help. Sometimes the student will be sufficiently embarrassed to cease complaining.

7. **I wish I knew some students would attempt to enlist me in disputes with other instructors or the administration.** On occasion, a student might say, "Do you think that an instructor should . . . ." This is usually a tip that you are not being asked a rhetorical question but are being asked to side against a position taken by another instructor. Similarly, you may hear grumbling during breaks or before class about another instructor or about the program administration. If

asked about another instructor or administrator, consider responding, "It is not appropriate for me to comment about anyone's class but mine. I would not appreciate another instructor making comments about my class and therefore I never comment about anyone else's class." When I hear rumors and grumbling, I usually call the program administration and try to give a "heads up" that a problem may be brewing. The program office can often then defuse the issue before it becomes a difficult problem.

8. **I wish I knew some students would over-rely on the Internet.** Many students are very proficient at using the Internet. Because so many cases and statutes are now accessible on reputable Internet sites, many students resist going to the law library and prefer to use the Internet to do research whenever possible. I have also discovered that a few students have "cut and pasted" materials from the Internet directly into their assignments. In one instance, a student used significant material from the ACLU website in a final project (with no attribution). The university held an honor board hearing to determine the appropriate penalty for the honor violation. Some paralegal programs require students to sign honor code pledges at the beginning of the program. Others require students to sign honor code pledges on each assignment. In any event, make sure your policy regarding the use of the Internet to do assignments is clearly stated.

9. **I wish I knew it was okay not to know everything**. I think I am a better teacher now than I was when I was first starting. I think I was so eager to do a good job, I became defensive if a student pointed out that I had misspoken or that I had made an error. It took me a bit of time to realize that it's okay not to know everything.

When a student points out that I have made an error, I try to respond, "Thanks. Great catch. Sorry I misspoke," and then move on.

Useful Web Sites for Teachers

- **http://honolulu.hawaii.edu/intranet/committees/FacDevCom/guidebk/teachtip/teachtip.htm**

This excellent site has information regarding "the first day," "dealing with stress," "preparing a course syllabus," and other useful teaching tips, including tips on learning students' names and faces quickly.

- **http://www.ntlf.com/html/lib/bib/names.htm**

This site provides twenty-seven ways to remember students' names.

Another excellent source of practical advice is found in Anita Tebbe's publication *Strategies and Tips for Paralegal Educators*, published by West Group (Thomson Delmar Learning), 610 Opperman Drive, St. Paul, Minnesota 55164. Note that this publication is now out of print.

THE LAW LIBRARY

Because legal research and writing is a "hands on" experience, students spend a good deal of time working on written assignments at a law library for most research and writing classes. The assistance and support of the law library is critical to the success of any legal research and writing course.

Law Library Tour

Most students benefit from a brief tour of or orientation to the law library before assignments begin in earnest. Ask the law librarian at the law library most students will be using if tours are given. If the law library itself does not offer tours, ask if you can conduct one for your students. Most law libraries are quite accommodating and are happy to provide or allow tours so long as the group is not so large as to be a distraction to those using the law library to work and study.

You may be able to schedule a law library orientation on the Saturday before classes begin. The law library is usually quiet at that time, allowing for a leisurely pace and a thorough question period. The only disadvantage to giving the tour before classes begin is that announcements such as "these are the Decennial Digests," or "West's Southeastern Reporter is located here" are largely meaningless to new students. On the other hand, simply gaining familiarity with the law library, its reserve room, reference area, and photocopiers is useful.

Alternatively, you may wish to wait until after the first few class sessions for the orientation. By this time, students may have done a bit of exploring in connection with other classes and may be a bit more familiar with the sets of books they will be shown.

If a law library tour is not practical or is not permitted, try to obtain pamphlets from the law library regarding its collection, policies, and hours. Many pamphlets include diagrams or floor plans of the library, which will be useful in pointing out the location of the various materials and sources. If a pamphlet is not available, consider preparing a one-page diagram of the law library layout and include the hours and telephone number of the library.

Some law libraries have meeting rooms or conference rooms and students may be able to use these rooms to meet and confer on projects or assignments.

Ask the law librarian if you can have copies of books being discarded so you can bring them to class and show students what books such as U.S.C.A. or Am. Jur. 2d look like.

Working with Law Librarians

Most law librarians will appreciate being informed of the activities of your class. Consider providing a copy of your course syllabus and assignments to a reference librarian so he or she will be able to anticipate what books or tools the class will be using. Some law libraries will designate an individual to serve as a contact for the paralegal students and this contact person will be primarily responsible for responding to questions and concerns.

Stay in touch with the law library. Some law school libraries arrange their hours and schedules around the activities of the law students, and as soon as final exams are over, will shift to a reduced schedule, often with little advance notice.

On occasion, a student may become overly reliant on a law librarian and may ask for help before fully exploring all of the options available to locate an answer. While most law librarians are very helpful, it can be frustrating for them to be asked for help before a student has made a diligent effort to solve a problem. Encourage students to seek help when it is needed, but remind them that once "on the job," they may not have any help available and thus they should learn as soon as possible to work on research tasks independently. You may wish to try to be at the law library to be of assistance a few times each semester so students can call on you for help, particularly for difficult assignments.

Some law libraries have meeting or conference rooms and you may be able to hold class on occasion at the law library. This is useful for demonstrating how to use certain books, such as digests and citators.

Other Law Libraries

If several law libraries are available in your area, obtain their hours and telephone numbers so students may attempt to research in other, perhaps more convenient, locations. Because it is difficult to know exactly which sets of books are available in several law libraries, I have usually announced that I prepared the assignments at "X" library so I *know* all answers can be obtained there. I then encourage students to "scout out" other law libraries if they wish but state that I cannot guarantee they will be able to obtain all answers to all assignments anywhere other than at "X." Several times during the course of the semester I ask students which law libraries they are using and ask them for their opinions as to layout, book availability, and assistance at these other law libraries. Over the course of a semester or two, you can get a fairly good idea of which other law libraries in the area maintain the books you will have your students use for their assignments and projects.

SUGGESTIONS FOR ASSIGNMENTS

Introduction

Because the heart of a legal research and writing class is the actual research and writing, I rely exclusively on research and writing exercises, assignments, and projects. I do not give any exams, although I have seen several useful multiple choice exams designed to test students on their knowledge of the features of various sets of books. If desired, exams can be a combination of true/false and multiple choice questions. Alternatively, exams can present a factual question and then ask students to explain how they would go about finding the answer to the question and to describe the research techniques they would use. A concise Test Bank is found in the last section of this Manual.

As to reading assignments, these are set forth in the syllabus and students are asked to read the text assignment for a class before that class.

The assignments for the first several chapters are exercises requiring the students to use sets of books to which they have been introduced in the corresponding text chapter. Because most people learn best by doing, students will need to locate and examine various sets of books to determine answers to questions.

In real-life situations, research is not always confined to such a question-answer approach. Often several issues need to be researched for a project and the answers are not always clear cut. Students will become ready for such complex assignments by preparing the more thorough writing projects, such as correspondence, memoranda, and briefs. On the other hand, paralegals are often asked quick research questions, such as, "How many directors must a corporation have in this state?" or "What is the statute of limitations for bringing an action for breach of a written contract?" These questions require a paralegal to consider which set of books will yield the quickest answer and then use the set to locate the correct answer. The assignments given in the first few chapters are designed to introduce students to sets of books they will be expected to be familiar with so they will be able to respond to "real life" research requests. These first several assignments are thus very practical in nature and are intended to encourage efficient and accurate research habits.

Similarly, the questions asked in the "State Your Answer" section for each chapter are designed to replicate "real life" assignments in law office settings. Whenever possible, these questions relate to topics discussed in the respective chapter so that, for example, after the discussion of the federal and state court structures in Chapter Two, students must locate information about their state courts by accessing Internet sites that will prove useful to them once they are employed.

Uniform Format of Assignments

Assignments are easier for instructors to review and grade if they all look alike. For this reason, consider providing each student with a photocopy of the assignment and asking that the answers be written directly on the assignment sheet. You may wish to suggest that students make a copy of the assignment sheet and use this as a work copy and transfer their answers to the "clean" copy before turning it in. You will then have a readable assignment and the students will have an extra copy of the assignment to refer to during class discussion of the assignment.

Duplicate copies of the assignments that are given at the end of each chapter are provided in this Manual so that if you prefer to photocopy these assignments and distribute a uniform version of the assignment, you may readily do so. Answer keys are provided in the same format, to make grading easier. Students should be encouraged to maintain "clean" copies of the bigger writing projects to use as writing samples for job interviews.

State Specific Assignments

The end-of-chapter assignments provided in the text require the use of federal or general texts far more than state-specific sets. The state-specific questions tend to relate to the larger, more populous jurisdictions, such as California and New York, because sets of books from these jurisdictions are available in many law libraries.

It is nearly impossible to draft assignments that will be suitable for students from every state. Moreover, students without access to larger law libraries may be unable to locate books from states other than their own. Thus, a much heavier reliance is given to questions requiring the use of federal or general texts such as U.S.C.A. or Am. Jur. 2d rather than those requiring the use of state specific sets.

I generally try to have students also use at least a few sets of books from states other than the one in which I teach. In this way, they get an overview of arrangements from other states and they will not feel lost or unprepared if they relocate to another jurisdiction. You are encouraged to modify the state specific questions so that students perform research using sets of books from your state as well as using those from other states.

Depending on your locale, you may want to focus on certain areas of law. For example, students in the Washington D.C. area benefit from additional instruction in administrative law and legislative history while students from northern California may appreciate assignments in the field of intellectual property and students from the Pacific Northwest may appreciate assignments relating to environmental issues.

The "State Your Answer" questions at the end of each chapter are often state-specific. For example, in Chapter Six, students are asked to access the Internet and determine how many times their state has cited the Restatement of Torts as of March 1, 2003 and what law reviews from their state are available on the Internet. The "State Your Answer" questions are intended to test state-specific research techniques and Internet research techniques because these are the types of questions paralegals are often asked in real life employment settings.

Timeliness of Assignments

The first semester I taught, it never occurred to me that students would not turn in assignments or projects on time or that the day (or evening) before a long-term project was due, students would ask for an extension. After consulting with several other instructors and my program director, I enacted a policy to penalize late papers. I am still not altogether happy with my policy and occasional grumbling exists. Nevertheless, I feel confident that the policy is fair and that no one student is being given some benefit or extra time that others are not.

Over a period of time, I also learned (the hard way) that the policy was best committed to writing in order to avoid misunderstandings. The late policy is fully explained in the first class session and is set forth in the syllabus. A paper is "late" and is subject to a penalty if it is not on my desk when I begin the class session. I explain to the students that deadlines are a way of life in the legal profession and they must begin to learn to complete assignments in a timely manner. I also explain that it is unfair to the majority of students who turn projects in on time if I allow another student extra time to complete an assignment.

Whether you enact such a policy is, of course, entirely discretionary. After years of teaching, I can only say that it has worked well for me and I believe it has taught the students to work with deadlines.

At one point, I allowed students to turn in assignments to me via facsimile. This turned out to be a disaster because both my law firm and program office were inundated with assignments (and a jam up of the fax machine) for several hours before a class started. Some instructors allow students to submit assignments via e-mail and some programs assign e-mail accounts to their instructors for that purpose. New educational software products, such as Blackboard, provide easy and convenient ways for instructors to communicate with students, post syllabi and assignments, remind students of deadlines, answer questions, accept assignments, and maintain grade registers.

I would suggest that if you elect to adopt a policy on late papers, enforce it uniformly. Once any exception is made, the integrity of the policy is compromised, and I have steadfastly (although reluctantly) refused to waver, even when presented with notes from doctors, employers, and even a congressman, explaining the situation that caused the delay. Clearly, however, exceptional circumstances may exist, and in the event of hospitalization or a death in the family, the program office has accepted late papers.

Finally, one unexpected benefit of a policy on late papers is that the number of latecomers to class is greatly reduced, thus eliminating distraction both to me and to the other students.

Grading Assignments

I try to grade the assignments and return them to the students as soon as possible. The longer writing projects take a great deal of time to read, however, and these often take two weeks to grade. In any event, I return one big writing project before the next one is due so that if a student is having some particular writing or citation problem, it may be addressed and corrected before the next project is due. As time consuming as it is, try to include comments as well as a grade so students can determine what parts of the project you thought were handled well and what parts showed weakness or lack of clarity.

Assigning grades to the smaller library assignments is fairly easy and straightforward. Each answer will be worth a certain number of points, which may be predetermined by you. These may vary from 10 points allocated for the first one or two assignments, which are very easy, to 30 to 40 to 50 points for the later, more complex assignments. I usually award extra points for answers found in pocket parts. Thus, if students do not have the right answer because they forgot to examine the pocket part, they are penalized more harshly. The lesson is usually quickly learned, however, and students seldom make the mistake of neglecting the pocket part twice.

Because new pocket parts and supplements are always being added to the sets, it is possible that a student will arrive at an answer different from that shown on an answer key. I explain to the students that it is entirely possible than an answer they have located is correct and I am simply unaware of it. Thus, if they provide me with some "proof," usually consisting of a photocopy of the page of the book from which they obtained their answer, I will give them credit.

Grading the bigger writing projects is considerably more difficult because it is nearly impossible to have a pre-determined point schedule in mind. Most instructors review projects from both a research and a writing perspective so that even if a project is well-researched and draws the right conclusions, failure to write clearly or to follow the basic principles of grammar and sentence construction will result in a lower grade.

In many instances, I create a somewhat unusual name for the "parties" in a matter, such as "Dr. Andersen" rather than "Dr. Anderson." When a misspelling of the party's name occurs, I automatically deduct five points and remind students that if one misspells the client's name, it will attract more attention than anything else in a law firm product. Similarly, using the word "statue" rather than "statute" is an automatic five-point deduction.

On occasion (and with a student's permission and without identifying the author), I have read aloud sections of projects that were particularly well written so other students can get an idea as to what the better projects were like. The bigger projects are typically worth considerably more points than the library assignments because they require students to exercise both their research and writing skills.

With regard to citation form in the bigger projects, I usually expect an occasional error in spacing, punctuation, and so forth. On the other hand, if the majority of citations are incorrect, or if the writer *never* includes the pinpoint cite for a quotation, I usually deduct several points. For the sake of convenience in averaging, I have graded the bigger writing projects in five-point increments (80, 85, 90, and so forth) because this seems to make more sense than a grade of 83 or 92.

Some paralegal programs have grading scales (90 to 100 is an A, and so forth) while others allow instructors to determine the scale. If you are allowed discretion in determining the scale, you might consider checking with schools and universities in the area for ideas on setting the scale. I currently follow the guidelines for Georgetown University. Some paralegal programs do not issue grades and the program is Pass/Fail or Pass/Fail/Honors. In many ways, these systems take the pressure off the competitive instincts many students have and allow them to focus more on learning than on collecting points.

Citation Form for Assignments

I do not require *Bluebook* form for the early assignments. While I demonstrate the correct format for cases, statutes, and so forth in the appropriate class and encourage students to begin learning good citation habits, I only require that the students locate the right answer. Deducting points for incorrect citation form so early in the class causes many incorrect answers at a time I am trying to build confidence and allow students to have some fun in the law library. While each chapter of the text provides examples of citation form for the authorities discussed in that chapter, citation form is not fully analyzed unless Chapter Eight. After I have thoroughly explained citation form in Chapter Eight, I then usually require *Bluebook* form for answers to assignments.

Book Crunches

One of the difficulties in assigning legal research projects is that many students must use the same sets of books. Often students will neglect to reshelve the books or may even misshelve books so that latecomers will have a difficult time locating the sources needed to complete their research tasks.

If you are in a locale in which there are several law libraries, students will invariably spread out among these other facilities after the first week or so. Try to encourage the use of other libraries by providing addresses and phone numbers for the other libraries in your area.

If there are fewer libraries in your area, and many students who must complete the same assignment, there will be some book crunches. In such cases, consider the following alternatives:

- **Books can be placed on reserve.** While placing books on reserve helps alleviate book crunches, it creates artificiality because the point of a research class is to learn to find materials. In "real life" situations, the books needed will never be collected and set aside in one convenient location.

- **Alternate assignments can be given.** Half of the students can be given assignment "A" while half can be given assignment "B." This will reduce problems encountered in the library regarding accessibility of books. The two drawbacks to this alternative are that it requires significant effort on the instructor's part to draft and then grade two separate assignments and there will inevitably be some grumbling that the assignment for one group was easier than that for another.

- **Allow students to work in pairs or small groups.** Students invariably compare notes and discuss research tips and strategies. In many ways, this brainstorming fosters and stimulates learning. Many instructors encourage this type of collegial attitude because it builds rapport among the students and sets the stage for the sharing of ideas that occurs in law office settings.

Because students will be working with each other anyway, to reduce the problems of unavailability of books, you could consider allowing groups of two or three to work together on an assignment. The disadvantage to this method is that some students may "coast" and allow others to do most of the work.

- **More time can be allotted for assignments.** To spread out the time during which students will be using the books, more time could be allotted to each assignment, perhaps two weeks for each chapter exercise rather than one. This approach may make life difficult for the instructor, however, because assignments will "pile up" and the instructor will move on to new material without being assured students have mastered previous topics.

Miscellaneous

- **Conferences**

If possible, you may wish to set aside a class session or two for student conferences. Particularly before a big project is due, students may have the need to meet with you to ask questions and review information. Generally, the last class session before a significant project is due is a convenient time for one-on-one student conferences.

- **Drafts**

Many instructors have students submit drafts of writing projects before a final project is due. The instructor then makes comments on the drafts and the students revise accordingly and turn in the final project as revised. In many ways, this approach duplicates real-life law office situations in which projects are given to a supervisor who makes comments and editing changes and the paralegal then revises as instructed. The disadvantages are that reviewing drafts leads to additional work for the instructor and "grade creep" because almost all students will receive high grades after following the instructor's directions. Moreover, it can lead to grumbling among students, who may say, "I did exactly what you wanted and I only got a B." Nevertheless, reviewing a draft may be a useful process for at least one project so students can become familiar with your demands and style.

- **Extra Credit**

Some instructors allow students to submit additional assignments to receive extra credit and boost their grade. Others believe that allowing students to provide additional assignments penalizes students who worked diligently and conscientiously on the first assignment. Moreover, extra credit assignments take additional time to prepare and then grade. When students have asked me if they can complete extra credit assignments, I usually explain that I do not grade additional assignments for credit, but that I have several older assignments they can complete and turn in to me for correction (but no additional credit) so that they can ensure they have mastered the material.

- **Mini-Memo**

Some instructors assign a "Mini-Memo" to students at the conclusion of the information presented on secondary sources (or at the conclusion of the information presented on citation form and citation validation/updating). This allows a brief glimpse as to students' writing abilities and also allows students to use all of their research skills to find an answer to a problem. Typically, this memo consists of one fairly straightforward issue and is limited to just a few pages in length.

- **Page Limits**

Consider imposing page limits for bigger projects. Otherwise, you may receive 20 and 30 page projects. Imposing page limits is commonly done by courts so imposing page limits in class may be good "real life" preparation for students who have difficulty being concise.

- **Final Projects**

If several projects are due for various classes at the end of a semester, creating a crunch and high stress for students, you may wish to consider having students drop their final projects off at your program office or mail them to you several days after the "official" last class. This allows students a few extra days for preparation of their larger projects, although it reduces the time available for grading to instructors who are often required to submit grades by a certain date. Students can be encouraged to provide a self-addressed and stamped envelope so you can return their projects to them after they are graded. Students can then revise the project accordingly and use it as a writing sample if a potential employer requires one.

CHAPTER BY CHAPTER RESOURCE INFORMATION

For each of the 19 chapters of *Legal Research and Writing for Paralegals* (4th ed. 2005), this Manual will address the following topics:

- Chapter Theme
- Classroom Discussion Approach
- Assignments (and Discussion of Assignments)

Chapter One: Finding the Law

Chapter Theme

The focus of Chapter One is to present background information on law libraries and to introduce students to the sources of law and the classification of law books as primary or secondary authorities and to provide an overview of the major law book publishers.

Because students will spend so much time during the course of a legal research and writing class in a law library, they should be given as much information as possible about law libraries in the area. If your paralegal program is affiliated with a certain law library or has an arrangement with a specific law library, you may wish to have the law librarian attend the class session discussing Chapter One and provide information about library hours, services, and policies.

An overview of *stare decisis* will generally stimulate class discussion because the concept of following precedents to promote stability and yet reversing or overruling precedent to accommodate change to meet society's needs is interesting and thought provoking.

A brief introduction to the primary sources (cases, constitutions, statutes, and to a degree, administrative regulations) "sets the stage" for the weeks to come which will then focus specifically on these authorities. Because beginning researchers often place greater emphasis than is wise on secondary sources, emphasis on the binding and mandatory nature of primary sources is useful.

Because many classes that follow will compare features of books published by West Group ("West") with those published by others, an introduction to West and other law book publishers is useful. If may be important to point out the evolving landscape of law book publishing as various companies merge with or are acquired by others. For example, many authorities continue to state that the publisher of U.S.C.S. is Lawyer's Cooperative Publishing although U.S.C.S. is now published by LEXIS Publishing.

Finally, although Chapter One (and the succeeding chapters) identifies various Web sites, you may wish to defer discussion of and even discourage use of the Internet for legal research (other than the "State Your Answers" questions) at this early stage of the learning process. Many instructors find that once students realize they can locate much information via the Internet, students become reluctant to use the law library and wrongfully assume that the Internet will provide them with all the material they need to perform legal research. The resulting projects written by these students are "flat" and lack analytical depth.

Classroom Discussion Approach

Because the material in Chapter One will likely be presented in the first class session, students may be somewhat hesitant about participating in class discussion. To break the ice, consider spending the first 20 to 30 minutes of class discussing some of the "housekeeping" for the semester. Introduce yourself, give information about the law library, discuss the text, distribute the syllabus, review the semester's schedule, and discuss grading and assignments.

To encourage discussion, you may wish to ask students what law libraries they are familiar with and what their impressions are of other law libraries. To try and get to know the students, you can ask each student to introduce himself or herself. You may ask if any students work in a law firm or law department or have any law-related background. Instructors who teach in large cities often have students in class who have been practicing attorneys in other countries and who wish to take a paralegal course to become familiar with the American legal system. These students often offer interesting comments about their legal systems and traditions and these comments serve as a springboard for discussing the differences between common law and civil law legal systems.

Students are often eager to discuss the conflicting goals in our legal system of promoting stability and yet fostering needed change. You may wish to discuss recent cases that demonstrate such change and ask for comment and reaction. For example, simply asking for students' "gut reaction" to the 2001 decision by the United States Supreme Court allowing disabled golfer Casey Martin to use a golf cart while playing in PGA sponsored events or the recent cases relating to the removal of Floridian Terri Schiavo's feeding tube will likely stimulate a lively class discussion.

Assignments

The first library assignment is designed for one purpose: to get students into a law library so they can readily find legal authorities if proper citations are given. Almost all of the students will get all of the answers correct on the assignment for Chapter One and this will build confidence. You will need to demonstrate the components of a citation, so that students understand that a case citation is always made up of several "standard" elements, such as a volume number, the name of a set, the page on which the case begins, and the date of the decision.

You may wish to substitute some questions requiring students to look at cases from your jurisdiction for some of the questions relating to cases decided by the United States Supreme Court.

The "State Your Answer" questions are designed to show students the breadth of information they may obtain by using the Internet and to illustrate how easy it is for them to locate the nearest federal depository library, and so forth.

Chapter Two: The Federal and State Court Systems

Chapter Theme

Chapter Two focuses on the federal and state court systems. Most students are unfamiliar with the organization of the federal courts. Once they understand the structure of the federal court system, they will be better able to evaluate cases they read, realizing that cases decided by any of the United States district courts are trial court cases, while cases decided by the United States courts of appeal are appellate court cases entitled to greater weight than trial court decisions.

Introductory information regarding federal court jurisdiction is provided. Although students will likely receive much more detailed information on this topic in their civil litigation or civil procedure class, a brief introduction may be helpful. Moreover, there may be some students who are taking only isolated or select courses, and this may be the only information they receive relating to this topic.

Classroom Discussion Approach

Students typically enjoy learning about the federal court structure and are particularly interested in the United States Supreme Court.

Students who work in or have worked in law offices may wish to discuss projects they have worked on, the process of appealing a case, or the lengths of time and costs involved in taking a case to an appellate court.

Some students may have participated in small claims court actions as litigants and are often eager to share their experiences. Some may have prevailed as plaintiffs and yet been unable to recover a judgment from a "judgment proof" defendant and may wish to discuss how they attempted to collect a judgment. The topic "how many appeals are necessary to ensure justice is done?" stimulates enthusiastic discussion.

Individuals who have worked in a court clerk's office or at a courthouse may participate by describing their duties and how these have changed to keep up with increasing litigation. Ask students what suggestions they have to reduce the caseload of courts or to expedite the appeals process. Should the function of granting "cert" be handled by another court? Should more specialized courts be established to serve as courts of last resort for certain matters, such as labor law cases, education cases, or social security cases?

Discuss the results of the first assignment and remind students that court reports are more than mere collections of cases as decided by courts. The books provide numerous helpful features, including tables of cases, names of counsel, and so forth.

Assignments

The second library assignment is straightforward and should be easy to complete. Students are directed to the sets of books that include decisions from each of the federal courts. You will need to demonstrate the citation abbreviations for *Federal Supplement* and *Federal Reporter*.

The intent of the assignment is to ensure students automatically make the mental connection between the name of a set of books and where the cases in that set fit into a court structure. The goal is for a student to see a citation to "F. Supp." and then immediately think, "trial case, lowest court in the federal system," so that citations and annotations to cases are not read merely as references to cases, but are read for context, enabling students to make informed decisions as to which cases to retrieve and read.

You may wish to add a few cases from your state and those from other states as well so students can get a glimpse as to how state court cases are published.

The "State Your Answer" exercise for this chapter is designed to show students the vast amount of information available at their fingertips, including state court statistics, maps of the federal circuits, and the like.

Discussion of Assignment

In reviewing the library assignment for Chapter Two, note that a "tricky" question was included, asking students to identify the Attorney General of the United States at the time a case was decided. This information is listed in the front of the volume of *United States Reports*; however, Janet Reno, who was previously serving as U.S. Attorney General resigned, and at the time the specific case was decided, John Ashcroft had taken her place, requiring students to note this information (provided by an asterisk reference) and then compare the date of decision with the date of appointment. Many students get the answer to this question incorrect, setting the stage for a discussion as to the importance of every word, punctuation mark, and asterisk in legal materials and the need to be very detailed. This "trick" question may teach students the need for careful examination of legal materials and the dangers of rushing through the information.

Chapter Three: Statutory Law

Chapter Theme

The focus of Chapter Three is on the procedure by which statutes are enacted, the publication of statutes, and the research techniques used to locate statutes. Just as most students are unfamiliar with the structure of the federal and state court systems, most students benefit from a refresher relating to the process of lawmaking. This process ties into the information relating to legislative history discussed later in Chapter Ten.

Once students are reintroduced to the procedure by which laws are enacted, they will be ready to learn about the publication of statutes and the advantages of annotated codes. After a discussion of the features of the annotated codes, students will be ready to use these features to locate statutes.

Because a discussion of the process of enacting, publishing, and locating statutes for each state is beyond the scope of the text, the emphasis of Chapter Three is on federal statutes. Moreover, because the procedure of enacting, publishing, and locating state statutes is nearly identical to that for federal statutes, less time can be devoted to state statutes.

Classroom Discussion Approach

Some students may have been involved to some degree in the legislative process and may be eager to discuss their experiences. Some may have worked as interns or staffers for legislative representatives or committees. Some may be aware of private legislation. Many may have contacted legislative representatives to ask for copies of bills or some other assistance.

Students sometimes have difficulty in understanding the fact that U.S.C.A. and U.S.C.S. are competitive sets and that ordinarily one conducting research would use one set or the other, but not both. Moreover, most law firms can only afford to buy one set. Consider refraining from giving an opinion as to your preference for which set to use. Stress that the assignment for statutes will require students to look at both U.S.C.A. and U.S.C.S. and that the following class session will include a discussion of the students' preferences after using both sets.

To stimulate discussion, ask students why an annotated version of a code would be more helpful than an unannotated version. Ask when an unannotated version might be consulted (for example, to obtain a quick answer to a straightforward question, such as how many extra days a party has to answer interrogatories if the interrogatories are served by mail). Ask the names of the two legislative bodies in your state. Discuss some legislation of general interest for which committee hearings are ongoing or which may be in conference. Encourage students to access the home pages of the U.S. Senate and House of Representatives or to access THOMAS (http://www.thomas.loc.gov) on the Internet to review debates occurring on the floor of the House or Senate.

Assignments

The library assignment for Chapter Three is the first true research assignment in that it requires students to locate the answers to certain questions with little or no guidance. Students are directed to use U.S.C.A. and U.S.C.S. so they can begin to appreciate both the differences and the similarities between the two sets. When instructed to use a specific set, students should do so because there is no assurance the answer can be located elsewhere.

Questions are phrased so that students will be readily able to identify whether they have found the correct answer. For example, if a question asks whether under the Eighth Amendment the denial of warm food is unconstitutional as cruel and unusual punishment, the annotations will use language nearly as identical as possible to the question. The assignment requires students to use pocket parts to locate some answers. Consider awarding an extra point or two for answers located in pocket parts. Those who forget to review the pocket parts and are penalized for it seldom make the same mistake twice.

You may wish to add or substitute a few questions requiring students to use the code from your state so they become familiar with its organization, indexing, and features.

The questions asked in "State Your Answer" require students to use the Internet to obtain information about their U.S. and state representatives and to locate a state statute (namely, to give the definition of "corporation" used in their respective states). As noted earlier, once students discover they can locate statutes on the Internet, they may become reluctant to use the law library, so a word of caution may be in order so they understand that effective researchers use both conventional print sources and digital sources to help clients.

Discussion of Assignment

In reviewing the library assignment for Chapter Three, you may wish to note that this assignment is very difficult and approximates the level of difficulty one may encounter in "real life" research situations when one researches statutes. Ask which students prefer U.S.C.A. (or U.S.C.S.) and ask if they can articulate a reason why.

Remind students that some answers could only be found by using a pocket part. Ask which questions were particularly difficult and whether any students developed any strategies for finding statutes more easily.

Chapter Four: Case Law and Judicial Opinions

Chapter Theme

Chapter Four introduces students to case law. Students will learn that not all cases are published and that the cases that are published share certain features. You may wish to show how these elements appear in the case reports by showing an old advance sheet to the students or by reviewing the case reproduced in Chapter Four of the text. Reviewing actual published cases is especially helpful to show how to locate pertinent portions of cases using headnotes.

Students often have a bit of difficulty understanding the designation of cases as "official" and "unofficial," and explaining this may require a comparison of a case in an official set with its publication by West in a regional reporter.

After the publication of state cases is discussed and students are familiar with the framework and units of West's National Reporter System, the publication of federal cases is discussed.

Star paging is explained so students will know how to convert citations and page references in *Supreme Court Reporter* and *Lawyers' Edition* to citations to the *United States Reports*, to comply with *Bluebook* and *ALWD* citation rules.

Students are introduced to the features included in West's sets of books so they may readily use the Table of Cases or Table of Statutes Construed.

Finally, once students are thoroughly familiar with how and where cases are published and the elements of reported decisions, case briefing is explained.

Classroom Discussion Approach

Ask students why or when a dissent or concurring opinion may be issued. You may consider discussing the current trend of U.S. Supreme Court justices to issue more concurring opinions than in previous years and ask what reasons students can think of why this has occurred. The "fractured" nature of the United States Supreme Court opinion in 2000 in *Bush v. Gore* may provide a good "jumping off" point for this discussion.

Discuss the policy reasons underlying the decision not to publish all cases (and the current controversy regarding whether unpublished cases can be relied upon) and why trial court decisions are rarely published.

Discuss the differing writing styles seen in cases, from the flowery and archaic styles of some writers to the terse and spare approach of others. Ask students if they have any tips to offer on reading and comprehending cases and stress how the features provided by the publishers (case synopsis, headnotes, and so forth) make reading cases somewhat easier.

Discuss the enhanced access of the public to cases now available on the Internet and discuss the effect of such ready availability on the public's understanding of our legal system in general and on law book publishing. If cases are available on the Internet, for free, why should law firms spend money to buy a set of case reports?

Assignments

The end-of-chapter assignments for Chapter Four include a library assignment designed to require students to locate and use the features seen in case reports (such as the Table of Cases, star paging, and so forth) as well as a case brief. The library assignment for this chapter is considerably less demanding than the assignment for statutory research given in Chapter Three because it is designed merely to familiarize students with the elements of cases and the features found in books reporting cases.

While a citation to a case is included for the case brief (*PepsiCo v. Redmond*), and a sample brief for the case is included in the Answer Key section of this Manual, feel free to substitute some other case, if desired. The case identified in the text, *PepsiCo v. Redmond*, is relatively short, involves an interesting trade secrets legal question, and yet presents complex reasoning. The briefs of this case should enable you to obtain a snapshot of your students' writing abilities that you have not been able to see from the library assignments previously given. The case may provide an excellent topic for discussion and students are typically enthusiastic about discussing this case(and the rights of employers to protect their valuable information versus the rights of employees to have job mobility and freedom to work) in the class after they have read and briefed it.

Suggestion for Oral Presentation: As a break from written assignments, you may wish to break students into two groups, one of which will argue FOR the use and citation of unpublished cases, and the other of which will argue AGAINST the use and citation of unpublished cases. Students may work in groups and make oral presentations in class.

The "State Your Answer" questions demonstrate how students may locate court reversal rates and locate court rules on the Internet.

Discussion of Assignments

Review the library assignment and case brief for Chapter Four. Most students do very well on the library assignment for Chapter Four because it is straightforward. Point out any common errors made by students in the case briefs and consider asking students to discuss some of the policy reasons underlying the *PepsiCo* decision (namely, the rights of employers to protect the investment made in senior employees and their valuable trade secrets).

Chapter Five: The Use of Digests, Annotated Law Reports, and *Words and Phrases*

Chapter Theme

Chapter Five completes the discussion of primary authorities by describing the use of digests, which are used to find cases. Additionally, students are introduced to A.L.R., which forms a bridge between the primary authorities (in that it publishes cases) and the secondary authorities (in that it publishes comment about those cases). Finally, a description of West's set *Words and Phrases* is included. This set also helps locate cases – specifically, cases providing the definition or interpretation of certain words or phrases.

I have found that explaining the format and use of digests is somewhat difficult. If at all possible, try to obtain an old copy of an advance sheet for a state or regional digest because its digest entries may help in the explanation process. More than almost any other topic, students will learn the most about digests by examining them in the course of doing the assignment for this chapter. Once the students have actually examined the digests, they will readily be able to understand their use and value.

Consider focusing on the most comprehensive digest set, the American Digest (or Decennial) System. Once students understand how this set works, they will easily be able to comprehend the smaller state-specific, court-specific, or regional digest sets because they are all organized the same way.

A.L.R. is a much easier set of books to understand because there is a conventional index to the set that is used similarly to other indexes. The section on A.L.R. is also related to the discussion in Chapter Six on encyclopedias because the encyclopedias routinely provide references in their footnotes to A.L.R. annotations. Similarly, when one Shepardizes or KeyCites a case, Shepard's and KeyCite will provide a reference to any A.L.R. annotation mentioning the case. You may wish to note the somewhat odd method of updating annotations contained in A.L.R. and A.L.R.2d, namely, the requirement of using a separate source rather than a pocket part to update the material in the main volumes.

Words and Phrases is also easily understood because it is as easy to use as any dictionary. Note that the assignment requires use of the pocket part in *Words and Phrases* in addition to the main volume.

Classroom Discussion Approach

Students usually have several questions regarding the use of digests and I have found that they do not fully understand the use of digests until almost all of the material is presented. This material often seems to be bit like a puzzle and the picture is not clear until the last piece is placed into the puzzle.

You might consider stressing that A.L.R. annotations are like finding "free research." If an annotation has been written about a topic, it will usually provide a complete analysis of that topic, enabling a researcher to obtain a thorough overview of an issue in one source.

To stimulate discussion, ask:

- In what circumstances would a researcher use the American Digest System rather than a state-specific or regional digest?
- When would the use of *Words and Phrases* be indicated?
- How often would one review an annotation in A.L.R. or A.L.R.2d (the earlier sets)?

- Why is it necessary to update annotations appearing in A.L.R. or A.L.R.2d?

Assignments

The library assignment for Chapter Five requires students to use several types of digests: the American Digest System, a regional digest, and a jurisdiction-specific digest. You may wish to require use of the digest from your state. The questions range from the easy ("What topic and key numbers is *Trecom Business Systems, Inc. v. Prasad* digested under?") to the more complex ("What topic and key number discuss lethal injection as a mode of execution in death penalty cases?").

The questions relating to A.L.R. are somewhat difficult and students are required to update the answers found by using pocket parts.

While there is only one question requiring the use of *Words and Phrases*, it also requires students to use the pocket part, reinforcing the rule that if a volume includes a pocket part, it must be examined.

Because the sets mentioned in Chapter Five are not available on the Internet, the "State Your Answer" questions require students to access West Group's website and retrieve information about the sets discussed in the chapter. Familiarity with this information may be helpful to paralegals in employment settings because they may well be required to assist law librarians or work with West representatives.

Discussion of Assignment

Review the library assignment for Chapter Five and discuss the organization and use of digests. Ask students if any difficulties were encountered using A.L.R. or *Words and Phrases*. Consider noting that the assignment requires the use of both the main volume and the pocket part of *Words and Phrases* and that if students failed to use the pocket part for the set, they will not obtain all the points available for this assignment.

Chapter Six: Encyclopedias, Periodicals, Treatises, and Restatements

Chapter Theme

Chapter Six introduces students to the four best-known secondary authorities: encyclopedias, periodicals, treatises, and Restatements. Most of these sets are easy to use because they are accessed by alphabetically arranged indexes either contained within the set itself (such as the indexes to the encyclopedias) or separately published indexes (such as those for legal periodicals).

Remind students to use encyclopedias not only for general information about a research problem but as a back-up for their other classes. For example, if a student is having difficulty understanding concepts such as venue or promissory estoppel in other classes, or has missed a crucial class, he or she should use an encyclopedia to gain additional information about class topics.

Consider bringing to class an issue of a periodical from a bar association to which you belong so you can illustrate the sophistication of some of the periodicals. Their practicality is easily contrasted with the academic nature of law reviews. Some law libraries will give you the older, soft-cover law reviews as they are replaced by hardback volumes. If you belong to any specialized legal associations or subscribe to any legal newspapers, bring some issues of their publications to class. Remind students that if they have ever used the *Reader's Guide to Periodical Literature* to do high school or college term papers, they already know how to use the *Index to Legal Periodicals & Books*.

Students may already be familiar with some treatises from other classes they are taking. These texts are easy to describe and use and should present little difficulty.

The Restatements, on the other hand, are often a bit more difficult for students to understand and their indexes can be hard to use. Students taking a torts class will perhaps be familiar with the Restatement (Second) of Torts and will be able to appreciate the function and value of the Restatements.

Perhaps the most critical thing for students to understand about these secondary sources is that no matter how reputable a secondary authority is, it is never binding on a court, and thus students should let the secondary authorities direct them to the primary authorities, which, if on point, must be followed.

Classroom Discussion Approach

So that students can determine which secondary sources should be consulted in the course of a research task, ask the following questions:

- When would an encyclopedia be consulted? How would a court or adversary view a brief containing only references to encyclopedias and no citations to cases or statutes?

- Why do individuals publish articles in law reviews and journals? Are some law reviews more respected than others? Why?

- Why do individuals publish articles in bar association or other association journals? Would a reader expect an in-depth treatment of a topic in a bar association publication? Why or why not?

- How does an author of a treatise (such as Prosser) develop a reputation? How is a beginning researcher to know which treatises are viewed favorably by courts?

- Why do courts cite the Restatements? What does this indicate about the effect and value of the Restatements?

Remind students that while many articles and periodicals can be found on the Internet, it may be difficult to determine the credibility of the article or author, unless the article found on the Internet is a duplication of one found in a well known law review or journal.

Assignments

The library assignment for Chapter Six requires students to use both C.J.S. and Am. Jur. 2d. By using both sets, students will be able to see the more thorough and comprehensive references to cases found in the footnotes in C.J.S. You may wish to include questions requiring students to use a local encyclopedia if one is published for your state.

The questions relating to legal periodicals require students to locate periodical articles by using the three most common research approaches: by subject matter or topic, by name of author, and by name of case.

The questions relating to treatises focus on well-known treatises that researchers are likely to encounter. Only a few questions are included for Restatements because researchers are more commonly directed to Restatement sections by other authorities in the course of their research efforts rather than initiating research in the Restatements themselves.

The questions asked in the "State Your Answer" exercise are designed to demonstrate the ease of finding academic information (namely, law journal articles) on the Internet and to demonstrate how widely accepted the Restatement positions are.

Discussion of Assignment

When reviewing the library assignment for the chapter, ask students what sets of books they found easy to use and which seemed more difficult to access. Ask for comments comparing and contrasting the various indexes students have seen in the course of their research efforts thus far. Discuss the fact that many of the cases one is referred to by the encyclopedias are "old." Discuss the relatively "worn out" look of many of the Restatements and the somewhat difficult-to-use Restatement indexes. Discuss the ease of being able to access indexes for periodicals by topic, author name, or case name. Discuss why law reviews from schools such as Harvard, Yale, and Stanford are the most frequently cited law reviews.

Chapter Seven: Miscellaneous Secondary Authorities

Chapter Theme

The focus of Chapter Seven is on the less well-known secondary sources, such as opinions of the attorneys general, law directories, and jury instructions.

If students are taking other courses in addition to Legal Research and Writing (for example, Civil Procedure or Litigation classes), they may already be familiar with some books, such as form books or jury instructions. Students often fail to appreciate, however, that such books can be used for legal research purposes. For example, both form books and books containing jury instructions will include the elements of causes of action. These books are often annotated as well so researchers can easily locate cases through these sets.

Uniform laws, when adopted, have the effect of statutes; until adoption, however, they are secondary sources and are thus discussed in this chapter relating to various secondary sources.

At the conclusion of this chapter, students will have been introduced to all of the sets of books they will need to know in order to perform most research tasks. The section on looseleaf services in Chapter Seven is related to the discussion on administrative law legal research found in Chapter Ten.

Classroom Discussion Approach

Ask students if they have used any form books. Discuss how and when to make modifications to forms so they fit the particular circumstances of a case.

Discuss the many uses of *Martindale-Hubbell*, such as its sections on the laws of all of the states, the laws of some foreign countries, and its inclusion of some uniform laws and treaties. You may wish to comment upon *Martindale-Hubbell's* practice of rating attorneys and law firms according to legal ability and ethics. Discuss the use of *Martindale-Hubbell* in connection with job hunting and how to target a resume to the best individual in a firm or legal department, for example, to a fellow alum of one's college or an individual who belongs to a common association. Discuss whether *Martindale-Hubbell* will ultimately be supplanted by law firm Web pages.

Note the proliferation of legal directories on the Internet, providing students with easy access to information about attorneys, law firms, and legal departments.

Assignments

The library assignment for Chapter Seven is designed to introduce students to the features of the less frequently used secondary sources. In depth analysis of the books is not intended. An overview of the variety of information to be gained from these sets is the goal so students will have some passing familiarity with these books.

You may wish to substitute questions from form books or jury instructions for your state if they exist. If students are taking other courses, such as Securities Regulation or Labor Law at the same time they are taking Legal Research and Writing, you may want to have students review looseleaf services relating to these topics.

The questions posed in the "State Your Answer" section demonstrate the ease of finding definitions, uniform laws, forms, fees, jury instructions, and other practical and useful information on the Internet.

Chapter Eight: Legal Citation Form

Chapter Theme

Chapter Eight introduces citation form. Because students have previously been introduced to the primary and secondary sources, discussion of how to cite these authorities will fit into an already established framework.

Citation form is hard work. There is really no way to learn it other than to become familiar with the organization and quirks of *Bluebook* or *ALWD* rules and to keep working at it.

Consider advising students to read the first 35 pages or so of either the *Bluebook* or *ALWD* simply to obtain some insight into the way these citations guides are organized and present material.

Putting citation examples on a blackboard or overhead projector is useful for demonstration purposes. While I usually devote nearly three hours to citation form, I point out that students will be expected to know how to use the *Bluebook* (or ALWD) on the job and that it is impossible to discuss in class every citation problem that may occur. Paralegals are often "on their own" in performing cite-checking assignments, and thus the sooner they learn to rely on the *Bluebook* or *ALWD* and understand where needed information will be located, the better they will be able to perform.

Classroom Discussion Approach

Perhaps the most critical thing students need to know about the *Bluebook* is that the majority of examples in it show citation form for law review articles. Because paralegals rarely perform cite-checking for law review articles and primarily perform this task for court documents and memoranda, they must understand the differences in typeface conventions for these different purposes. Thus, a thorough understanding of the rule of the *Bluebook*'s Bluepages will be helpful.

If you use *ALWD*, note the many user-friendly features, such as the use of spacing guides, practice tips, Sidebars, and the like.

Another item worth discussing is the effect of court rules or even the idiosyncrasies of various legal writers on citation format. For example, many jurisdictions require (and many attorneys prefer) some citation form other than that shown in the *Bluebook*. Ask students what other citation forms they have seen. Be familiar with local rules, if any, relating to citation form so you can provide this information to students.

Discuss the various software programs that enable researchers to check some elements of citation form (accuracy of pages, dates, volumes, and so forth) in documents.

Discuss why a uniform system of citation is important and what poor citation form says about the author of a project. Consider comparing errors in citation form to spelling errors. While readers may understand a misspelled word, spelling errors obstruct clarity and generally cause the reader to think poorly of the author.

Assignments

The assignments for this chapter require students to correct citations according to the rules of the *Bluebook* or *ALWD*, as preferred by you or your program. I have found that many students perform quite poorly on these assignments, even when nearly identical examples are shown in class or in the text. This may result from an inattention to detail and a reluctance to devote the time and effort needed to perform the difficult task of cite-checking.

In grading these assignments, consider whether you will mark the entire answer incorrect if any portion of it is incorrect or whether you will allocate points to various segments of a citation. Many instructors prefer to mark the entire answer incorrect if any portion of it is incorrect because it is nearly impossible to apportion points for giving the correct case name, underscoring it, following it with a comma, including the proper abbreviations, showing the correct spacing, and providing the correct parenthetical. While this approach is strict, it does approximate "real life" and conveys the following two messages to students: citations are either right or they are wrong – there is no middle ground; and citation form is important.

The citations in the assignments to be corrected are fictitious. Students will be able to complete these assignments without going to the law library. You may wish to decide whether all assignments subsequent to these must reflect proper *Bluebook* or *ALWD* citation form.

I have found that there is no significant difference in class grades when the citation form assignments are done in class or when they are given as "take home" assignments. There are advantages and disadvantages to each method: if the exercises are to be completed in class, some students will invariably forget to bring their *Bluebooks* or *ALWD*s that day and are at a disadvantage; if the exercises are "take home," some students will lack the confidence to complete them on their own and will rely on the assistance of others.

Once you have corrected the citation form assignments, consider putting the correct answers on the blackboard or using an overhead projector in your next class so that students can easily see what mistakes they made and ask questions. Reviewing the answers one by one will reinforce citation rules.

The "State Your Answer" exercises in this chapter are designed to allow students to become familiar with the websites for *ALWD* and those relating to universal citation format because these sites will be useful to them once they secure paralegal positions.

Chapter Nine: Updating and Validating Your Research

Chapter Theme

While case updating and validating can be explained in a narrative form, as in the text, an actual demonstration of the techniques of Shepardizing and KeyCiting are worth the proverbial one thousand words. If at all possible, try to obtain an old copy of a *Shepard's* advance sheet so you can show students how to look for volume and page numbers when Shepardizing the old fashioned way, namely, using books.

To demonstrate Shepardizing online or KeyCiting, it may be possible to use computer facilities at your school or law library, or, alternatively, representatives of LEXIS and West may be willing to come to class to demonstrate their products.

Like star paging, Shepardizing/KeyCiting is one of those tasks that if students think they understand it while in class, they will easily be able to perform it once they have the pertinent books or computers at hand. Similar to star paging, Shepardizing and KeyCiting are entirely self-correcting. Recommend that students who are unsure they are updating correctly access the cites to which *Shepard's* or KeyCite refers them so they can verify that their updating techniques are accurate.

Remind students that Shepardizing manually (using actual print materials) is rapidly becoming a thing of the past. Many law firms no longer subscribe to *Shepard's* in print form and all legal professionals in such an office with Shepardize/KeyCite online. The advancements in software programs that automatically extract citations from a document and then print the results of updating make learning to Shepardize manually nearly outdated. Nevertheless, learning to Shepardize manually teaches students what signals to look for, the significance of the treatment of a case, and provides a solid foundation for Shepardizing online or KeyCiting.

Classroom Discussion Approach

Ask students what advantages there are in Shepardizing/KeyCiting early in the research process. What are the risks of Shepardizing/KeyCiting the day before a brief must be filed? In what ways can *Shepard's*/KeyCite serve as research tools?

Discuss the duty to Shepardize/KeyCite all primary authorities and the effect of a failure to Shepardize.

Discuss the advantages and disadvantages of Shepardizing manually as opposed to Shepardizing online or KeyCiting.

You may be able to write or contact LEXIS Publishing (www.lexis.com) and West (www.west.thomson.com) and ask for copies of marketing materials describing and explaining Shepardizing and KeyCiting. LEXIS's Web site offers a quick review of the judicial opinions and quotations from those opinions that have stressed the legal duty to Shepardize and criticized lawyers for failing to do so.

Assignments

The assignment for Shepardizing is relatively straightforward and students should perform well. Consider explaining to students that it may be better for them to perform well on the Shepardizing assignment than on the citation form assignment because citation form can be mastered on their own with time and effort. If, on the other hand, students leave a paralegal program without understanding how to Shepardize, this task may not be able to be mastered independently.

Consider whether the answers to the questions for this assignment must be given in correct *Bluebook* or *ALWD* form. Requiring only that students reproduce what they see in *Shepard's* and not be required to use *Bluebook* or *ALWD* form may reduce stress; however, requiring that the answers be in correct citation form, while time consuming for students, will reinforce citation skills and also require the use of other research skills, such as those involved in locating parallel citations.

The Shepardizing assignment requires that students not only Shepardize cases but also Shepardize statutes and a treaty so that they are introduced to the many sources that can and must be Shepardized.

The assignment for Chapter Nine covers only Shepardizing manually. The assignment given at the end of Chapter Twelve (on LEXIS and Westlaw) includes questions relating to Shepardizing online and KeyCiting.

The "State Your Answer" exercise for Chapter Nine asks students to review West's and LEXIS's websites and review descriptions of their products. Students are also asked to review an article comparing and contrasting *Shepard's* with KeyCite.

<u>Discussion of Assignment</u>

Review the assignment for Shepardizing and obtain students' reactions to using *Shepard's*. Ask students who may have Shepardized online or KeyCited to compare and contrast online case validating with the manual method of Shepardizing. Ask what problems, if any, students encountered in Shepardizing. Consider asking whether there is any value in learning to Shepardize using conventional print volumes, or whether Shepardizing and KeyCiting online have eliminated any need for familiarity with the print volumes of *Shepard's*.

Chapter Ten: Special Research Issues

Chapter Theme

Chapter Ten provides an overview of specialized research tasks that may not be encountered by paralegals on a routine basis.

Each of these tasks is slightly complicated by the fact that the books used to perform the research and arranged and indexed differently from the conventional sources students have already used.

The intent of this chapter is not to provide a comprehensive and exhaustive treatment of the topics of legislative history, administrative law, international law, or municipal or local law. It is merely to introduce these topics to students and provide some ideas as to sources to consult if students encounter these research issues. Students may take separate courses in legislative history, administrative law, or international law, and this chapter merely provides basic information regarding the research tools used to obtain information relating to these topics.

Classroom Discussion Approach

Ask students when a legislative history analysis would be helpful. Discuss some judges' reluctance to rely on legislative history in interpreting a statute. Discuss the ways in which technology, such as the THOMAS Web site, make compiling some elements of a legislative history easier now than years ago.

Ask students for examples of the way administrative agencies affect all of us. The topic of administrative law often results in enthusiastic discussion as students consider the wide-ranging effect administrative agencies have and yet how little most of know about the way the agencies operate and are staffed. Discuss some of the criticisms of the agencies for promulgating their own rules and regulations and then holding hearings and issuing decisions relating to alleged violations of those rules and regulations. Ask if any students have ever complained to an agency about television or radio content, air travel issues, or advertising. Consider the additional work of agencies such as the FTC and SEC, which must now also be alert to false advertising and stock fraud occurring over the Internet.

International law is another topic that should provoke lively discussion. Ask students why countries comply with their treaty obligations. Discuss the effectiveness of international tribunals, such as the International Court of Justice, and why their decisions are often ignored.

Ask students if they have ever attended a city council meeting or watched one on public access television. Those students from smaller towns can discuss the open nature of local government due to the fact that meetings are well-publicized in the local paper and because proposed and final ordinances are published as well, enabling citizens to become actively involved in the democratic process.

Students who work in law firms may wish to discuss some of the requirements imposed by local court rules relating to papers filed with courts. Discuss the effect of technology and whether e-filing is available in your jurisdiction for pleadings and motions. Some courts now require lawyers to submit disks of their briefs so the court can verify word counts. Such disks often provide an easy way for courts to review voluminous files with many exhibits, and many documents include hyperlinks for immediate access to pertinent exhibits and cases cited in briefs.

Assignments

The library assignment for Chapter Ten requires students to examine some of the better known sources and texts for compiling legislative histories and for performing research in administrative and international law.

Some law libraries maintain much of their legislative history materials in new media such as microfiche, and you may want to make sure conventional print sources are available or are placed on reserve for students to use.

Small law libraries may not have all of the international materials needed to complete the assignment from the textbook and you may need to make appropriate substitutions. No questions relating to municipal law are included because you may wish to include some questions requiring the use of the city or country code from your jurisdiction.

Only a few questions are included for each topic addressed in Chapter Ten because the focus of the chapter is simply to familiarize students with these less commonly used research sources so they will know which books to consult if they need to perform any of these specialized research tasks.

The "State Your Answer" exercise is intended to encourage students to begin familiarizing themselves with the wealth of materials available on the Internet, including in-depth information relating to legislation, presidential documents, agency information, C.F.R., municipal ordinances, and court rules.

Discussion of Assignment

Discuss the library assignment from Chapter Ten. Ask which of the topics researched (legislative history, administrative law, or international law) proved to be the most challenging. Discuss how interesting reviewing the *Congressional Record* or *Weekly Compilation of Presidential Documents* can be. Discuss the somewhat "abbreviated" nature of the index for C.F.R. as compared to the very thorough and "forgiving" indexes such in U.S.C.A. and U.S.C.S.

Chapter Eleven: The Digital Library: LEXIS, Westlaw, and Non-Print Research Sources

Chapter Theme

Chapter Eleven is intended to introduce students to some of the newer technologies available to researchers (excluding the Internet, which is the subject of Chapter Twelve). Many students will be available with microforms, CD-ROMs, and computers. Others may not be so familiar and may, in fact, be intimidated by some of the technologies.

The primary emphasis of Chapter Eleven is on computer assisted legal research, specifically, the use of LEXIS and Westlaw. While Chapter Eleven provides some basic information about these two research systems (and some others as well), and while both LEXIS Publishing (or its parent Reed Elsevier) and West publish helpful brochures and handouts, there is no substitute for "hand on" learning on the computer systems.

Determine whether your law library will provide formal training for your students so they have an opportunity to formulate queries, use the new natural language searching capabilities, Shepardize or KeyCite online, locate cases and statutes, and explore the incredible variety of materials available on LEXIS and Westlaw. LEXIS and Westlaw may offer training sessions in your area or may be able to provide speakers to guest lecture for you and share some research tips and techniques with your students.

You may wish to require that your students access the various online tutorials offered by LEXIS and Westlaw.

Classroom Discussion Approach

Ask students to describe their experiences with the varieties of technologies discussed in Chapter Eleven. Most will have used microfilm or microfiche. Many students who have not used LEXIS or Westlaw will be sufficiently familiar with computers in general to discuss common issues such as signing on and off, using a password, downloading, and printing.

Ask students to list advantages and disadvantages of conventional legal research techniques and research using newer technologies. Consider the following questions:

- Would it be easier to locate a topic name and key number by using the Descriptive Word Index to one of West's digests or by using Westlaw?

- Would it be easier to Shepardize using bound volumes of *Shepard's* or by Shepardizing/KeyCiting online?

- Would a small firm or a large firm best benefit from access to LEXIS or Westlaw?

- Can computers give a researcher too much information?

- What is the future of LEXIS and Westlaw if more and more material is made available for free on the Internet? What is the future of conventional print publishing?

- Is there a market for commercial fee-based Internet providers? Why would legal professionals pay for materials that, for the most part, are often offered for free?

- What will LEXIS and Westlaw need to offer their subscribers who may be wooed away by the Internet?

- How do economic realities often dictate the choices of which sources to use?

- In some instances might it be more efficient to use conventional print sources than computerized legal research systems to locate an answer to a question?

Mention the fact that clients are only billed for time expended on conventional legal research as opposed to the fact that clients are billed for time expended *and* computer time when research tasks are performed using LEXIS and Westlaw.

Consider advising students to start research projects by consulting conventional print sources and then when they have some general idea as to the issues involved in a project, to then turn to computer assisted legal research. Alternatively, for a first project on LEXIS or Westlaw, consider suggesting to students that after they have completed one of the bigger research projects (such as the brief or memo) by using conventional print sources, they then sit down at the computer and start all over again. This approach enables students to tell if their computer research strategies are effective because they will already know what cases and authorities they should be encountering. They will also be able to see the diverse and numerous authorities the computer services can locate – in some instances, so numerous as to be overwhelming.

The method of performing the very same research task by first using conventional sources and then online sources allows students to compare directly the advantages and disadvantages of conventional research techniques with those of using computer assisted legal research techniques.

Assignments

The library assignment for Chapter Eleven is designed to ensure students at least sit down in front of LEXIS and Westlaw and become somewhat familiar with each system and the vast array of information that can be obtained through computer assisted legal research. The questions asked are fairly straightforward and should not present any great difficulty. Questions include use of Shepard's online and KeyCite.

Some law libraries have prepared or "canned" exercises for using LEXIS and WESTLAW and you may wish to consider using these in place of or in addition to the assignment in the textbook.

The "State Your Answer" exercise for this chapter is fairly short and requires only that students review the LEXIS and Westlaw database coverage and identifiers.

Discussion of Assignment

After students complete the library assignment, discuss whether they have preferences for either LEXIS or Westlaw. Discuss and compare the process of Shepardizing online or KeyCiting with Shepardizing manually. Ask if students encountered any particular difficulties with computer assisted legal research.

Chapter Twelve: E-Research: Legal Research Using the Internet

Chapter Theme

The focus of Chapter Twelve is to introduce students to the Internet as another tool in their arsenal of legal research techniques. Some students may be fairly familiar with using the Internet to find cases and statutes while others may be familiar with the Internet but haven't used it to find legal resources.

To reduce anxiety, consider mentioning that it is not necessary for students to know what a "browser" or "search engine" is to conduct legal research on the Internet. Just as they may not know exactly how a microwave oven cooks food or how a radio produces sounds, it is not necessary to understand how the Internet works in order to use it.

The primary emphasis of this chapter is to ensure students understand the vast array of information available to them for free 24 hours each day. Cases decided by courts are available within hours or minutes, statutes can be located with a click of a keystroke, forms for preparing documents for filing with courts and agencies are available for downloading, and telephone numbers and addresses for court clerks are readily accessible. Additionally, substantive materials, such as articles from legal periodicals, are available. No student should leave a paralegal program without at least some understanding of how to access this information.

Classroom Discussion Approach

Like the classes devoted to instructing on Shepardizing online and KeyCiting and on the use of LEXIS and Westlaw, any class related to Internet legal research will be more effective if a "real life" demonstration can be included. I have generally asked my program office to provide me with a suitable classroom, screen, computer, and Internet access when I teach this class. Consider starting with just a few introductory remarks about the Internet, its history and use, and then ask students to sit at the keyboard and enter or key in various Web sites. Consider using the following as good jumping off sites: www.washlaw.edu; www.megalaw.com and www.findlaw.com. This method will demonstrate both the ease of use of the Internet and the variety of legal materials available to students.

Students who have already used the Internet for legal research will be eager to volunteer. Other students who have never used the Internet may need some prodding, but once they see how easy it is to enter the Web address, and then merely "point and click" to find information, they will become far more comfortable.

After several students have had the opportunity to look at Web sites and explore a variety of legal sites, discuss the credibility of various sites and the danger of relying solely on materials such as anonymous articles found on the Internet. Discuss the transience of some sites and the fact that often just as one becomes familiar with the look and feel of a site, it changes or disappears entirely.

Ask how the vast amount of material available for free 24/7 on the Internet will affect the publishers of conventional print sources and LEXIS and Westlaw. What will happen to sets of books such as *United States Reports* or *Federal Reporter* if researchers can give Internet citations in documents referring to these cases rather than being required to cite to the books themselves?

Teaching Tip

I have found that if I discuss the Internet too favorably and too early in my legal research classes, some students rely nearly exclusively on the Internet and quickly tire of the hassle of going to a law library. Their projects often lack in-depth analysis of a topic. It's a bit of a balancing act to ensure that students are well trained to use conventional print sources while also pointing out the many valuable uses of the Internet.

Assignments

The first assignment for this chapter is designed to ensure students sit down in front of a computer and explore various Internet sites. The questions are fairly easy and students should be able to find the answers quickly. The questions are intended to ensure students visit a variety of excellent Web sites, including Findlaw and THOMAS.

The "State Your Answer" questions also demonstrate the vast array of legal resources now available on the Internet, whether through so-called "legal sites" (such as FindLaw and MegaLaw) or through non-legal sites, such as Google. The non-legal sites are particularly helpful in obtaining information relating to clients (their official corporate names, their stock ticker symbols, and so forth). The last question (relating to the Oklahoma Association of Wine Producers) will show students how easy it is to become "seduced" by the Internet: The site appears credible and legitimate; yet it is a "fake" site.

Rather than use "State Your Answer" (which includes specific website addresses), you may wish to assign a "treasure hunt" and require students to find and print the following information and documents:

- The address and telephone number of the supreme court in your state;
- A form for incorporating a for-profit corporation in your jurisdiction;

- A map of the federal circuits;

- Biographical information for United States Supreme Court Justice Souter;

- A copy of 17 U.S.C. § 105;

- The Senate Office addresses of the senators from your state (using THOMAS);

- A copy of the Patriot Act (using THOMAS); and

- The first page of the United States Supreme Court case decided in 2001 relating to professional golfer Casey Martin.

Chapter Thirteen: Overview of the Research Process

Chapter Theme

The focus of Chapter Thirteen is to provide some guidance and tips to students on how to start and end a research project. Emphasize that some of the most valuable time spent on a research task is thinking things through. The Research Planner provided in Chapter Thirteen should help students develop an ordered and logical approach to research tasks as opposed to running directly to the law library and grabbing books. The Research Planner provided may help to remind students of the many sources that can be consulted.

Some students find research confusing and frustrating. This is often caused by a failure to take effective notes. Poor note-taking leads to numerous scraps of paper with jumbled sentences, half-completed conclusions, and incomplete citations. Explain that time invested in developing a system of note taking and in organizing notes will really pay off later when it is time to write.

Knowing when to stop researching is often troublesome for beginning researchers. Students are also inclined to ask, "How many authorities should I cite?" I never give a specific number because I do not want students to believe that research is like a recipe – that if you include the "right" number of authorities, the answer will be correct. Consider stressing that each project (and author) is unique and that eventually they will become more confident in their research techniques and will become comfortable with the uncertainty inherent in legal research.

Classroom Discussion Approach

The topics of getting started in research and knowing when to quit usually stimulate lively discussion because students are often eager to share their tips, strategies, and mistakes. Consider the following questions to provoke discussion:

- How do you get started?
- What set of books might you look at first if you had no idea what to do?
- How much time do you spend thinking about a project before you begin?
- What techniques have worked best for you?
- What techniques have been unrewarding – what would you avoid if you had some projects to do over again?
- Is there one set of books that is always helpful to you?
- How do you take notes? Do you use index cards, looseleaf sheets of paper, or some other technique?
- How do you stay focused on one issue at a time and avoid unproductive detours?
- What approaches can you take to obtain clear instructions from your supervisor?
- How do you determine when to stop researching?
- What part do/should economic realities play in determining the scope of a project?

Assignment

There is no library assignment for Chapter Thirteen. The "State Your Answer" assignment is intended to show students that information and tips on how to conduct research (as well as research tutorials) can be found on the Internet.

Chapter Fourteen: Back to Basics

Chapter Theme

The focus of Chapter Fourteen is to review certain basic principles of grammar, spelling, and punctuation. Many students routinely overestimate their abilities regarding these matters and can use a quick refresher of these topics.

Providing examples is the best way to demonstrate common errors. Collect samples that show common writing mistakes. Examples can be found in advertisements, newspapers, and anonymous student assignments from previous semesters. Ask students to be alert to writing errors and to bring into class examples they find.

Encourage students to supplement the text by purchasing books on grammar, spelling, and punctuation. Many books include exercises and questions and are readily found at almost any bookstore. Other assignments and exercises are available on the Internet sites mentioned in Chapters Fourteen and Fifteen.

Classroom Discussion Approach

Ask students if they believe they have difficulty spelling and what techniques they have developed to improve. Discuss the disproportionately negative effect spelling and grammar errors have on a reader. Discuss the expectations of a client who is paying significant sums for legal services and who receives documents that include errors. What is adverse counsel or a judge likely to think of such errors?

Consider giving an impromptu (uncollected) pop spelling quiz. Ask students to write down the following words (you may need to use them in sentences): judgment, license, privilege, acknowledgement, rescission, occasion, occurrence, affect, effect, liaison, defendant, decedent, principle (meaning rule), recede, succeed, accede, exceed, and supersede. Correct aloud in class.

Discuss whether computer aids such as Spell Check are helpful tools or mere crutches. What are students' experiences with grammar-checking software programs? What tools and books do students rely on to improve spelling, grammar, and punctuation? Discuss the numerous errors found in many "professional" publications such as newspapers and magazines.

Mention that most dictionaries include a section on commonly misspelled words, together with basic information on grammar and punctuation.

The discussion relating to grammar, spelling, and punctuation is usually quite lively, with students eager to share lessons they learned in previous classes. It is common to have students say, "I was always taught that . . . ." You may need to explain that in many instances, there is more than one correct way to spell a word or punctuate a sentence. Consider advising that in the legal field, one should likely err on the side of caution and stick to the most conservative rules relating to grammar, spelling, and punctuation.

Assignments

The end-of-chapter assignment for this chapter is in three parts: one for grammar, one for spelling, and one for punctuation. The exercises are straightforward but should give students an idea as to areas needing improvement. Students should be aware that many placement agencies use similar tools to test skill levels before placing a candidate in a paralegal position. Students may thus encounter similar tests when job hunting.

The "State Your Answer" assignment is designed to introduce students to two of the best websites for information on writing and grammar. The Government Printing Office reproduces its entire *Style Manual* on the Internet. The GPO *Style Manual* offers excellent information on grammar, punctuation, and spelling. Similarly, the Bartleby website offers sections of *The Elements of Style*, which is the "classic" guide to good writing. Students should be encouraged to "bookmark" these two sites for ready access.

Chapter Fifteen: Strategies for Effective Writing

Chapter Theme

The emphasis of Chapter Fifteen is on the five characteristics of legal writing: precision, clarity, readability, brevity, and order. Because the cornerstone of legal writing is communication, *effective* communication is a must. Tips and strategies are included to assist students in learning to communicate effectively and efficiently in their writing.

While the current focus in legal writing is the "plain English" movement, it is difficult to make students understand that effective legal writers work very hard to purge their writing of redundancies, jargon, and vague words. It is a constant campaign to persuade students that use of legalese (such as "hereinabove mentioned"), use of imprecision phrases (such as "this matter"), and use of redundant phrases (such as "each and every") can often be omitted and still result in a professional project.

Classroom Discussion Approach

Ask students why they believe those in the legal profession are so wedded to jargon. Is this a technique used to impress clients? Does it arise out of a misplaced notion that if individuals are required to pay hundreds of dollars for a letter, it should sound "legal" or scholarly?

Ask why it is difficult to be brief. How does one achieve brevity and yet not produce an abrupt or choppy project? Does "plain English" sound or appear unsophisticated?

Ask students to provide examples they have seen of legal jargon or redundant writing. Discuss the effect such writing has on a reader.

Urge students to compile form files of effective writing samples as they encounter them in their jobs.

<u>Assignments</u>

The end-of-chapter assignment for this chapter is designed to test the following fundamentals of effective legal writing: precision, clarity, readability, and brevity.

- To demonstrate the technique of precision, students must select the correct words to be used in a sentence.

- To demonstrate clarity, students must rewrite certain sentences containing elegant variation and negatives.

- To enhance readability, students must rephrase sentences in the active voice, use parallel structure to provide a list of items, and must reword sentences to avoid jargon.

- To achieve brevity, students must omit needless words and eliminate redundancies.

The "State Your Answer" assignment is intended to show students the excellent Internet sites devoted to writing. The SEC site gives numerous examples of writing in plain English. Purdue University's "Online Writing Lab" is well known for its excellent information. Finally, Professor Volokh's site is helpful in eliminating legalese.

Chapter Sixteen: Legal Correspondence

Chapter Theme

Chapter Sixteen introduces students to the different types of correspondence they may be expected to prepare. Consider bringing samples of non-confidential letters to class so students can see the format of letters written in law offices and legal departments.

Some students often insist on writing "like lawyers" and the tone of their letters will include archaic phrases and have a stuffy tone. Other students may to go the other extreme and produce letters that are far too informal and conversational in tone. One of the most difficult tasks in teaching writing is to communicate how to strike a balance between producing documents in "plain English" and yet achieving the formality required in business and legal writing.

Classroom Discussion Approach

Students generally like to discuss letter writing. Ask what styles they have observed that they believe are effective and what styles they have seen that are arrogant, patronizing, legalistic, or stuffy. Why and how did these problems occur? Ask students to bring in samples of letters they have seen that they believe are effective as well as samples of some that may be poorly written or failed to communicate information clearly to the recipient.

Discuss how "bad news" can be effectively delivered to a client. How can positive news be communicated to a client without resulting in a guarantee of success?

Assignments

The letter writing assignment included in this chapter is based on a type of corporation code statute that is common in all states because all states require a foreign corporation to qualify to transact business in a state before it begins transacting business. The letter is a combination of a "good news" and a "bad news" letter because the corporation in question did not violate the law in maintaining a bank account in the foreign state but did violate the pertinent statute by performing landscaping services in the state without first qualifying to conduct business.

In reviewing and grading the letters, common errors you may encounter include the following:

- Failing to include a reference notation, namely, the "Re:" line;
- Using an improper reference notation, for example, using the notation "Re: Outdoor Artists, Inc v. Mahony" when the matter has not yet proceeded to litigation;
- Failing to spell all parties' names correctly;
- Spelling "statute" as "statue";
- Failing to include a recitation (or complete recitation) of the facts;
- Failing to give the "bad news" that OA cannot sue Leo Mahony until OA qualifies to conduct business and that OA is liable for a civil penalty for failing to qualify when it should have;
- Failing to actually give an opinion or respond directly to the client's inquiry;
- Failing to recommend some course of action to the client.

You may wish to assign a letter writing project that requires students to conduct some research first and then draft a letter based upon that research. Other types of letters that can be assigned include the following:

- A letter in response to an advertisement for a job;

- A letter demanding payment of a debt owing to a client;
- A letter in response to a demand for payment; or
- A letter providing a client a status report on his or her case.

The "State Your Answer" exercise is designed to demonstrate to students the wide array of information available on the Internet relating to writing, and specifically relating to correspondence. Information is readily available regarding formatting, effective letter writing, and various tips to make letters more clear.

Chapter Seventeen: Legal Memoranda

Chapter Theme

The focus of Chapter Seventeen is to provide students with an overview of the process of preparing legal memoranda. Preparing a legal memorandum is a common task and one that requires both research and writing skills.

Students often have a difficult time maintaining objectivity – once they hear or see the words "our client," they tend to concentrate only on those arguments supporting the client and ignore any contrary authorities. The mission of a memo as an informative and explanatory document (rather than a persuasive document) must be continually emphasized.

The format of a memo is different from other legal documents, and you may wish to stress that while it seems awkward to set forth the questions to be addressed in question format on page one, this approach is critical because it provides an instant snapshot to the reader of the questions the case presents.

Classroom Discussion Approach

Ask students to imagine they joined a law firm or legal department two years after the commencement of a major case. What would be the best way to become familiar with both the positive and negative aspects of a case? Discuss the uses of a memo later in the life cycle of a case, namely, that it forms an excellent foundation for other documents (such as briefs and motions) and serves to alert everyone (including the client) to the weaknesses of a case so they can be anticipated and overcome.

Discuss whether clients should be provided copies of a memorandum that includes several arguments and sections that are contrary to the position the client wishes to assert.

Assignments

The memo-writing assignment given requires sophisticated research as well as writing. You may wish to substitute a "closed" memorandum, namely, one in which you provide citations to all of the cases and other authorities needed and students then prepare the memo based solely on the authorities you have provided.

In reviewing and grading the memos, be alert to the following common errors:

- Lack of parallel structure in the format of questions/issues.
- "Fudging" the statement of facts in favor of the client rather than presenting the facts in a neutral and unbiased manner;
- Failure to apply the legal rules found in cases to the facts of the memo (beginning writers are often inclined to merely summarize the cases they find rather than analyze what those cases mean for the client's specific factual situation);
- Failure to include sufficient facts from cases cited in the memo to enable the reader to understand how and why those cases apply to the client's particular problem;
- Providing legal conclusions without citing any supporting authority;
- Over-quoting (rather than analysis as to how and why those quotations are applicable);
- Errors in citation form;

- Failure to include descriptive headings and subheadings to alert the reader as to the topics to be addressed; and
- Overuse of personal pronouns, such as the following: "I would advise the client . . . ." or "I do not believe that . . . ."

The "State Your Answer" questions are intended to introduce students to some sites that may be of help in preparing memoranda. The information given on IRAC analysis and the use of thesis statements is particularly useful. Similarly, the website that discusses the functions of a legal memorandum is highly helpful.

Chapter Eighteen: Legal Briefs

Chapter Theme

The focus of Chapter Eighteen is to introduce students to briefs filed with courts. The elements of trial briefs and appellate briefs are discussed and compared. While all paralegals may not prepare appellate briefs, they may well be involved in other parts of the brief-writing process, such as preparing or reviewing the table of authorities or doing the cite-checking for the brief. Part of the body of a trial brief or appellate brief may be "cut and pasted" or "cannibalized" from other research projects, such as legal memoranda or other briefs and motions.

The use of the word "brief" in these several contexts (case briefs, trial court briefs, and appellate briefs) can be confusing and you may wish to review the purpose of case-briefing so students can readily understand how different case briefs are from trial court briefs.

Classroom Discussion Approach

Because the objective of a brief filed before a court is to persuade the court to rule in favor of one's position, discuss techniques to make writing more persuasive.

Discuss what judges will look for in briefs. Ask students to put themselves in the reviewing judge's place. What would a judge appreciate in briefs filed in his or her court?

Discuss the effect of a well-written statement of facts. Ask students if a table of contents or index to a brief can be persuasive. Discuss the placement of weak and strong arguments. What are the advantages of placing the strongest argument first?

Discuss the use of footnotes. Do they interrupt the flow of an argument or do they neatly remove confusing citations from a well-reasoned argument?

Assignments

There are two assignments for this chapter. The first assignment requires students to prepare a brief to be filed in a trial court. If students have been taking a litigation or civil procedure class, they will likely be familiar with the use and goals of a motion for summary judgment. If students have not been exposed to this motion, you may need to explain its purpose and effect.

The assignment included in the text is relatively easy to research. Thus, most of the time students will expend on the project can be devoted to writing. All of the authorities can readily be located by reviewing the annotations following the First Amendment in U.S.C.A. or U.S.C.S. The cases relied upon by the students may differ in some respects but most students should have no difficulty finding the most significant cases dealing with prayers at graduation: *Wallace v. Jaffree*, *Lee v. Weisman*, and *Santa Fe Independent School District v. Doe*. Shepardizing or KeyCiting these cases will lead to numerous law review/journal articles and A.L.R. annotations about this topic.

When the project has been handed in to you, you may wish to discuss in class the topics raised by the project. Most students are eager to discuss the cases they found and almost all will have an opinion on such an interesting topic as prayer in public schools.

Because paralegals are not usually involved in the actual drafting of appellate briefs, the second assignment relates to a task that they may typically be asked to perform: preparation of a table of authorities for an appellate brief. This assignment also serves as additional reinforcement for citation form.

The "State Your Answer" questions are designed to reinforce information about preparing briefs (such as strategies for effective brief writing and the use and power of persuasive headings) as well as to ensure students understand that they *must* comply with court rules relating to briefs and that finding those rules is easily accomplished through the Internet.

Chapter Nineteen: Postwriting Steps

Chapter Theme

The focus of Chapter Nineteen is on post-writing steps. At the end of a complex project, students are often so tired and exhausted they fail to put the final touches on a project by polishing it and proofreading it. These items are not mere details; they are an integral and important part of the writing process. Failure to proofread properly can result in a project that is legally correct but is so unprofessional no one will be informed or persuaded by it.

Consider emphasizing to students that every part of research and writing is a campaign. It is not sufficient to stand on solid legal ground. A writer must present a professional project. After hours of perhaps days of effort, a writer cannot afford to have a reader dismiss a project by thinking, "If I can't trust this writer to spell correctly and use proper sentence construction, how can I trust that the writer has correctly interpreted complex case law?" Emphasize that sloppy projects create poor impressions and can have devastating effects.

Classroom Discussion Approach

Proofreading is one of the most difficult tasks in legal writing. We become so familiar with our projects that we simply cannot see our errors. Ask students what techniques they use to proofread. Discuss why enthusiasm wanes at the end of a project and what can be done to revive interest. Ask students what their impression is of a writer who produces a messy or unprofessional project. What is a client likely to think? Discuss the low tolerance in law firms for careless errors. Discuss how to ask for and receive criticism of one's writing. Discuss how students can proofread the projects of others and deliver constructive criticism.

<u>Assignments</u>

The end-of-chapter assignment for this chapter is easy and straightforward. It is designed to make students focus on proofreading. Unfortunately, any assignment labeled "Proofreading" is somewhat artificial because students will be on the alert for errors. You may wish to have students complete this exercise in class so they are under some time constraints. It is impossible, however, to truly duplicate a "real life" scenario of proofreading at the end of a long day, interrupted by telephone calls, conferences, and office crises.

An alternative is to bring to class a three or four page document from your office that includes some common errors (in spacing, spelling, paragraph length, inconsistent numbering, and so forth). Students can be asked to proofread the document in class. Such a "real life" assignment will more closely duplicate what working paralegals are expected to do in law office settings.

The "State Your Answer" questions are intended to introduce students to proofreaders' marks (widely available on the Internet) and to reinforce the importance of being able to locate court rules relating to the formatting of documents submitted to those courts.

CONCLUSION

I have taught paralegals for more than twenty years in a variety of settings: professional schools, in-house seminars, in college programs, and in post-baccalaureate ABA approved programs. I have also practiced law and been involved in raising a growing family. As most teacher/lawyer/parents do, I have often thought: "This is too much. Something has to give." Yet when I think of scaling back my schedule, I never think of giving up my teaching. I find teaching an extremely rewarding and satisfying vocation. I love seeing the progress students make and while there are many days when the thought of grading any more papers is mind numbing, I am enthusiastic about the great accomplishments of my students.

I hope you find teaching as rewarding and challenging as I have and I welcome your comments, questions, and, of course, ideas for interesting assignments!

Sincerely,

Deborah E. Bouchoux

Summer 2005

Assignments and "State Your Answers" for All Chapters

Following are the Assignments for all chapters as well as the "State Your Answer" questions for all chapters. All of the Assignments and State Your Answers are in the same format as their answer keys, which follow in this Manual.

Instructors may easily copy the Assignments and State Your Answer sheets from this section of the Manual and then use the Answer Keys that follow when preparing and grading assignments. When Assignments and Answer Keys are in the same format, grading is easier.

Name _____

Assignment for Chapter One
(xx points)

1. a. Give the name of the case located at 531 U.S. 70 (2000).

   b. Who argued the case for the Petitioner? _____

2. a. Give the name of the case located at 447 U.S. 303 (1980).

   b. Who delivered the opinion of the Court? _____

   c. Who dissented? _____

3. a. Give the name of the case at 502 U.S. 301 (1992).

   b. Give the date the case was argued. _____

   c. Give the date the case was decided. _____

   d. Locate a case in this volume in which the defendant's name is *Bryant* and give the name of the case. _____

   e. Give the citation for the *Bryant* case. _____

   f. What part did Justice Thomas take in the *Bryant* case? _____

Name _____

State Your Answer – Chapter One
(xx points)

1. Use Table T.1 of the *Bluebook* or access http://www.ncsconline.org (the website for the National Center for State Courts) and locate and access your state's judicial website. Who is the current chief justice or senior judge of your state's highest court?

2. Access the site for the American Association for Law Libraries and identify the state, court, or county law libraries in your state or nearest locality.

3. Access the site for GPO Access and identify at least one federal depository library for your state or nearest locality.

4. Access Cornell Law School's Legal Information Institute at http://www.cornell.edu. Select "Lexicon" and provide the definition for *stare decisis*.

Name

Assignment for Chapter Two
(xx points)

1. a. Give the name of the case located at 531 U.S. 57 (2000).

   b. Give the holding of the case.

   c. During the period of time covered by the cases in the volume, which United States Supreme Court Justice was assigned or allotted to the Tenth Circuit?

   d. Locate a case in this volume in which the plaintiff's name is *Buckman Co.*

      (i) Give the full name and citation of this case.

      (ii) Who was the United States Attorney General at the time this case was decided?

2. a. Locate a case in volume 502 of the *U.S. Reports* in which the plaintiff's name is *Byers* and give the name and citation of this case.

   b. Give the result reached in this case.

3. To which circuits are the following states assigned?

   a. Utah   _____

   b. Connecticut   _____

   c. Missouri   _____

4. a. Give the name of the case located at 154 F.3d 161 (4th Cir. 1998).

   b. Which judge issued the opinion of the court?

5. a. Give the name of the case located at 33 F. Supp. 2d 78.

 b. Which of the United States District Courts decided this case?

 c. Who represented the defendant in this case?

_____
Name

State Your Answer – Chapter Two
(xx points)

1. Access the site http://www.uscourts.gov and review the map of federal circuits and districts.

    a. In which circuit is your state located?

    b. In which district court would you file a complaint for age discrimination?

2. Access the site for the National Center for State Courts at http://ncsconline.org and locate the "State Court Structure Charts."

    a. How many justices sit on your state's highest court? _____

    b. What are the names of your state's courts?

3. Within the site for the National Center for State Courts, select "Court Statistics Project" and then locate "State Court Caseload Statistics." Review Table 2. How many total cases (including both mandatory and discretionary petitions) were filed in your state's highest court?

Name_____

Assignment for Chapter Three
(xx points)

1. What title of the United States Code relates to Shipping?

2. Use U.S.C.A. and cite the title and section that govern the following:

    a. Research relating to lupus.

    b. Definitions of African elephants.

3. Use either U.S.C.A. or U.S.C.S. and cite the title and section that govern the following:

    a. Smallpox vaccines and vaccinations.

    b. Beer as being nonmailable.

4. Use the Popular Name tables as directed and cite the title and section for the following:

    a. Use U.S.C.A. and give the citation for the short title of the Sarbanes-Oxley Act of 2002.

    b. Use U.S.C.A. and give the citation for Jennifer's Law.

    c. Use either U.S.C.A. or U.S.C.S. and give the citation for the Boggs Act.

    d. Use either U.S.C.A. or U.S.C.S. and give the citation for the Muhammad Ali Boxing Reform Act.

5.   Use either U.S.C.A. or U.S.C.S. and describe the counseling available for veterans who are victims of sexual trauma.

6.   Use the U.S.C.A. volumes for the Constitution. Answer the following questions and cite the best case to support your answer. Give case names only.

   a.   Under the First Amendment (Freedom of Religion), does requiring mandatory chapel attendance for cadets and midshipmen at federal military academies violate the Establishment Clause?

   b.   Under the Eighth Amendment, is denial of warm food cruel and unusual punishment?

7.   Use U.S.C.A. Give an answer to the question and cite the best case to support your answer. Give case name only.

   a.   Under 18 U.S.C.A. § 1302, is "keno" a "lottery" within the meaning of internal revenue laws?

   b.   What encyclopedia reference are you directed to in order to better understand this statute?

8.   Use U.S.C.S. Answer the following questions and cite the best case to support your answer. Give case names only.

   a.   Under 29 U.S.C.S. § 152, are interns, residents, and fellows employed by medical centers "employees"?

   b.   Under 15 U.S.C.S. § 1052, may a trademark including the letters "U.S." prominently displayed be registered as a trademark?

9. Use *U.S. Statutes at Large*.

        a. What is the short title of Public Law 107-296?

        b. Give the citation for this law in *U.S. Statutes at Large*.

        b. What was its designation in the House of Representatives?

10. Use *U.S. Statutes at Large*.

        a. For whose relief was Private Law 106-14 enacted?

        b. What was the purpose of Private Law 106-5?

Name _____

State Your Answer – Chapter Three
(xx points)

1. Access one of the Internet sites for the United States Senate and identify your state's two senators.

2. Access the National Conference on State Legislatures (www.ncsconline.org) and select the appropriate topics and links.

   a. Identify the two legislative bodies in your state (one in Nebraska).

   b. Determine whether your state imposes term limits on its legislative representatives. If it does, describe those limits.

3. Use FindLaw (http://www.findlaw.com) to link to your state's statutes. Review the business organizations or corporations statutes for your state and give your state's definition of the term "corporation."

4. Use either the *Bluebook* or *ALWD* and determine which publisher (if any) publishes the compiled statutes in your state. Note that some states publish only officially and no publisher will be identified.

Name _____

Assignment for Chapter Four
(xx points)

1. Give the name of the case located at 667 N.W.2d 467 (Minn. Ct. App. 2003) and state what the case involves.

2. Use 39 P.3d. What case in this volume construes the meaning of "dwelling"?

3. Give the author of the opinion for the case located at 540 U.S. 544 (2004).

4. Use 710 N.E.2d. What case in this volume construes Mass. Gen. Laws ch. 272, § 17?

5. Locate the case at 846 A.2d 318 (D.C. 2004).

    a. Give the name of the case.

    b. What does headnote 7 discuss?

6. What is the name of the case located at 163 F.3d 238 (5th Cir. 1998)?

7. What is the name of the case located at 308 F. Supp. 798 (S.D.N.Y. 1970)?

8. What is the name of the case located at 679 F. Supp. 360 and which U.S. district court decided this case?

9. What is the name of the case located at 54 F.R.D. 282 (W.D. Pa. 1971) and briefly state the topic the case discusses.

10. In which National Reporter System series do the decisions of the following states appear?

        Kentucky

        Ohio

        Connecticut

11. Give the name of the case located at:

    a.   622 N.W.2d 1

    b.   272 S.E.2d 706

    c.   195 So. 248

12. Give the parallel citations for the case located at 116 S. Ct. 356.

13. Locate the case at 121 S. Ct. 447. How does page 39 of the parallel *United States Reports* begin?

14. Locate the case at 144 L. Ed. 2d 196. How does page 219 of the parallel *United States Reports* begin?

15. Use the *National Reporter Blue Book* (2005 Cum. Supp.) and give the parallel citations for the following cases.

    a. 252 Ga. Ct. App. 45

    b. 165 N.J. 205

    c. 167 Or. Ct. App. 1

16. Locate the case in 535 S.E.2d in which the defendant's name is *Traino*.

    a. Give the citation

    b. Who represented the appellant in this case?

    c. Who was the Chief Judge of the Georgia Court of Appeals during the period of time covered by this volume?

Name _____

State Your Answer – Chapter Four
(xx points)

1. Use either the *Bluebook* or *ALWD* and identify the names of the sets of books that report case decisions from your state's courts.

2. Use either the *Bluebook* or *ALWD* and prepare the following citation (assume it is being cited in an internal office memorandum at your firm):
    Anderson v. Diaz, a case decided by your state's highest court in 2003 and reported in volume 709, at page 404 of the relevant reporter.

3. Access the site for the Center for Individual Freedom (http://www.centerforindividualfreedom.org) and select "Legal" and review the statistics for the 2003 term of the United States Supreme Court. What was the reversal rate (expressed as a percentage) for your circuit during the 2003 term?

4. Access the site MegaLaw at http://www.megalaw.com and select "State Law." Locate the site for your state's courts or judicial system and determine which court rules can be accessed through your state's site.

Name
Assignment for Chapter Five
(xx points)

1. Use the Table of Cases for the *Eleventh Decennial, Part 1*.

   a. Under which topic and key numbers is the following case digested: *Trecom Business Systems, Inc. v. Prasad*?

   b. Give the citation to the case in which the defendant's name is *Derokey*.

2. Use the Descriptive Word Index to the *Eleventh Decennia, Part 1*.

   a. Which topic and key number discuss lethal injection as a mode of execution in death penalty cases?

   b. Look up this topic and key number in the *Eleventh Decennial, Part 1*. Which 1999 case from Arizona discusses this?

3. Use the Descriptive Word Index to the *Tenth Decennial, Part 2*.

   a. Which topic and key number discuss games as nuisances?

   b. Look up this topic and key number in the *Tenth Decennial, Part 2*. Which 1991 Nebraska case discusses this general topic?

   c. Which 1997 Rhode Island case updates this?

4. Use West's set *Federal Practice Digest, 4th Series*.

   a. Which topic and key number discuss a right to a jury trial in employment discrimination cases?

   b. Review this topic and key number. Which 2003 case from the Eighth Circuit ruled on this issue?

c. Review this case. Was the plaintiff entitled to a jury trial in this matter? Why or why not?

5. Use West's set *United States Supreme Court Digest*. Give the citations to the case *Bayne v. Wiggins*.

6. Use West's *Atlantic Digest*.

   a. Which topic and key number discuss the use of expert witnesses in battered women's syndrome cases?

   b. Review the topic and key number. Give the name of the 1981 Maine case that discusses this issue and tell whether the expert witness testimony was permitted.

7. Use A.L.R. *Quick Index* for A.L.R.3d, A.L.R.4th, and A.L.R.5th. Find and cite the annotations that relate to the following issues:

   a. Liability of a nursery school and day care center for injury to a child attending the facility (specifically, for injury caused by a crib).

   b. Liability of dog owners for emotional injuries sustained by persons frightened by the owners' dogs.

8. Review the above annotations, and answer the following questions:

   a. For 7(a) generally, which is the most recent case from the Georgia Court of Appeals in which negligence was established and the *res ipsa loquitur* doctrine was not at issue?

   b. For 7(b), cite a 1932 California Court of Appeals case that generally relates to this topic.

9. Use West's set *Words and Phrases*. What cases construe the meaning of the phrase "nurturing parent doctrine"? Give case names only.

Name _____

State Your Answer – Chapter Five
(xx points)

1. Access West's website at http://www.west.thomson.com. Select "Product Type" and then "Digests" and locate the digest for your state. Use the format "West's Iowa Digest" if you have difficulty. How often is your state's digest updated?

2. Access the site MegaLaw at http://www.megalaw.com. Use "State Law" to access authorities and information for your state. Review "State Government Information" for your state.

   a. Identify your state's lieutenant governor.

   b. Identify whether your lieutenant is a native of your state.

3. Access West's website at http://www.west.thomson.com.

   a. Select "User Guides" and then review a User Guide entitled "Using Secondary Sources." How does West describe A.L.R. on page 1 of this User Guide?

   b. Using the "Search Products" box, search for *Words and Phrases*. Review the product information about this set, specifically its "Summary of Contents." What words and phrases does Volume 37 (also called Book 86) cover?

Name _____

Assignment for Chapter Six
(xx points)

1. Use Am. Jur. 2d.

   a. Which volume, title, and section deal with gambling on sports events?

   b. Review this section. What exceptions exist to the federal statute prohibiting gambling on sporting events?

2. Use Am. Jur. 2d.

   a. Which volume, title, and section deal with chickens as nuisances?

   b. Review this section. Which Massachusetts case held that noises and odors from a chickenhouse and yard maintained in a clean manner are not a nuisance?

3. Use C.J.S.

   a. Use the Table of Cases. Under which topic and section is the case *Albertson v. Leca* discussed?

   b. Which topic and section discuss cruelty as grounds for divorce?

   c. Review the above section. What happens if both parties are guilty of habitual cruel and inhuman treatment?

   d. Give a short summary of the definition of "release."

131

4. Use *Am. Jur. Proof of Facts (3d)*.

   a. Give the citation to an article relating to the availability of punitive damages in an automobile accident with a school bus.

   b. Review the above section. What South Carolina case(s) discuss(es) this? Give the case name(s) only.

   c. Who authored this article?

5. Use *Index to Legal Periodicals & Books* to answer the following questions:

   a. Cite an article written by Ann Laquer Estin in spring 2002 relating to marriage.

   b. Cite an article written in late 2003 relating to end-stage anorexia and competence to refuse treatment.

   c. Cite an article published in the winter of 2002 about a case in which the defendant's name is *Gilmore*.

6. Use the Subject Index for *Current Law Index* for 2003 and give the citation to an article relating to school busing.

7. Give the title and the authors of the April 2003 law review article located at 81 Tex. L. Rev. 1177.

8. Use *J. Thomas McCarthy on Trademarks and Unfair Competition* (4th ed. 1992).

   a. What section discusses "puffing" as false advertising?

   b. Review the section. Is a claim that a product is "better" than another product false advertising? Why or why not?

9. Use *Williston on Contracts* (Richard A. Lord ed., 4th ed. 1990).

   a. What section discusses rejection of goods for defective quality?

   b. Review this section. May a buyer reject goods for deficient quality where the buyer has failed to provide specifications needed by the seller to determine and meet the alleged quality standards? Provide an answer and cite the best case in support of your answer.

10. Use *Restatement (Third) of Trusts*.

    a. What section discusses the removal of a trustee, generally?

    b. Review this section. How may a trustee be removed?

    c. Review the Reporter's Notes for this section (specifically, comment e). May a trustee be removed for habitual drunkenness in Ohio? Provide an answer and cite the relevant statute in support of your answer.

Name _____

State Your Answer – Chapter Six
(xx points)

1. Access the Web site for Georgetown University Law Center at www.ll.georgetown.edu. Select "Learn" and then "Tutorials." Review the information given on encyclopedias. Which of the two national or general encyclopedias does this site recommend as a starting place? Why?

2. Access the University Law Review Project at www.lawreview.org. Select "General Law Reviews." What law reviews from your state are now available through this site?

3. Access the Washington & Lee Law School study on the most cited legal periodicals at www.wlu.edu.library/research/lawrevs/mostcited.asp. Sort the table by rank. As of 2003, which were the top four most-cited periodicals? How many times was each cited?

4. Access the site of the American Law Institute at www.ali.org and review ALI's annual report for 2004. Review the table that indicates how many times published cases cite to the Restatements.

    a. How many times has your state cited the Restatement of Torts as of March 1, 2003?

    b. What is the most frequently cited Restatement in your state?

Name_____

Assignment for Chapter Seven
(xx points)

1. Use *Black's Law Dictionary* (8th ed. 2004).

    a. What is the definition of "motion to suppress"?

    b. What topic and key number are you directed to relating to this definition?

    c. What does the legal maxim *fructus pendentes pars fundi videntur* mean?

2. Use the most current edition of *Martindale-Hubbell Law Directory*.

    a. An attorney named Hugh L. Wilcox, Jr. is with the Florence, South Carolina firm of Wilcox, Buyck & Williams. Where and when did Mr. Wilcox attend law school?

    b. Review the Corporate Law Departments volume. What corporation employs Catrina McLean?

    c. An attorney named Philippe Beurier is with the Paris, France law firm Bredin Prat. Where did he receive his law degree?

    d. What is the filing fee in North Carolina for filing articles of incorporation for a corporation?

    e. Review the ABA Model Rules of Professional Conduct. What Rule relates to confidentiality of information?

    f. In China, how long does software copyright protection last?

    g. Review the Uniform Arbitration Act. What does § 13 cover?

3. Use *Am. Jur. Legal Forms (2d)*.

   a. What forms relate to the payment of moving expenses in employment contracts?

   b. Review the first form. What Am. Jur. 2d reference are you given?

4. Use *Am. Jur. Pleading and Practice Forms Annotated*.

   a. What form provides a complaint against a bar or tavern owner for an attack by an intoxicated mob?

   b. Review the complaint. What does Paragraph 1 allege?

   c. What form provides a complaint against a cosmetic surgeon for facial disfigurement?

   d. Review the complaint. What does Paragraph 7 allege?

5. Use *Uniform Laws Annotated*.

   a. Has Utah adopted the Uniform Probate Code (1969)?

   b. If so, give the citation to Utah's statute.

   c. Review the Uniform Probate Code. What is the general topic of section 2-907?

   d. Review section 2-907. Generally, is a trust for the care of a designated animal valid?

Name _____

State Your Answer – Chapter Seven
(xx points)

1. Access the Web site for the National Association of Attorneys General at http://www.naag.org and identify the attorney general for your state.

2. Access the online legal dictionary at http://dictionary.law.com and provide the definition for "nunc pro tunc."

3. Access the Web site for the National Conference of Commissioners on Uniform State Laws at http://www.nccusl.org/update/AboutNCCUSL_desktopdefault.aspx and identify the commissioners from your state.

4. Access MegaLaw at http://www.megalaw.com and select "Legal Forms" and then "Secretary of State Forms." What is the filing fee in your state for filing articles of incorporation (to incorporate a business) for a stock or "for profit" corporation?

5. Access the article "What is the Law? Finding Jury Instructions" at http://www.llrx.com/columns/reference19.htm and determine whether your state's jury instructions are available online.

Name

Assignment for Chapter Eight
(xx points)

There is at least one thing wrong with each fictitious citation below. Correct the citations using the current edition of the *Bluebook* or *ALWD*. You may need to supply missing information such as dates. Punctuation is not needed after the citations. Assume you are preparing a memorandum in your office and unless otherwise indicated, assume that the citations appear in textual sentences rather than as "stand alone" citations. There is no need to include "pinpoints," unless otherwise directed.

1. Vincent Amato, Jr. v. Randall F. Cochran, a 1990 Rhode Island Supreme Court case found in volume 601 at page 224 of the relevant reporter.

2. Anderson General Construction Company v. Candy Benner, a Michigan Supreme Court case decided in 2001, located in volume 664 at page 14.

3. Michael J. Finnegan versus Teresa Finnegan, a 1994 case from the Georgia Court of Appeals, located in volume 607 of the relevant reporter, page 903, with quoted material on pages 914 to 916.

4. Douglas Consolidated Corporation vs. Flynn Brothers, 502 United States Reports 16, 329 Lawyers' Edition (Second Series) page 789, 319 Supreme Court Reporter page 906.

5. Federal Communications Commission v. Anne Griffin, Richard Garcia, and Diana Francois, 145 Federal Reporter (Third Series) 886.

6. USA v. Mark Gage, Trustee, 114 Federal Supplement (Second Series) 423, decided in the District Court for the District of Columbia.

7. Gunther Association v. Andrea Chu, a 2003 Supreme Court case.

8. Title 42, United States Code, Sections 2244 through 2248.

9. Title 15, U.S.C.A. Section 109.

10. Title 35 U.S.C.S. Section 1561(a).

11. Section 15-455 of the Idaho Code.

12. Section 22-013 of Maryland's Health Occupations Code.

13. Fourth Amendment to the United States Constitution.

14. Section 3-211 of Restatement (Second Series) of Contracts.

15. An article by Kelly Gray and Richard P. King entitled "Calculating Loss of Consortium," published in volume 42 of the South Carolina Law Review, at page 1054, with a quotation from pages 1062 through 1068.

16. Volume 6, Section 14:10 of the second edition of the treatise authored by Kevin Bidwell entitled "A Practitioner's Guide to Family Law."

17. Assume the following case is cited in a brief to a Massachusetts state court that requires parallel citations: Reynolds v. Patty Shaw, 309 Massachusetts Appeals Court 109. Give the correct citation.

18. Assume the following citation appears as a "stand alone" citation: the 2004 United States Court of Appeals case from the Third Circuit entitled Reynolds Restaurant Division Inc. v. Northern Maintenance Management Company. Give the correct citation.

19. The definition of "negligence" appearing on page 450 of the current edition of Black's Law Dictionary.

Name

Memorandum Assignment for Chapter Eight
(xx points)

There are numerous errors in the fictitious citations in the following brief memorandum. Correct citation errors using the current edition of the *Bluebook* or *AWLD*. You may need to supply missing information.

The general rule is that shareholders of a corporation receive dividends when and if declared by the board of directors acting in its discretion. Allen Association v. Taylor Corporation, 523 U.S. 16 (1998). Thus, the determination to distribute dividends is a discretionary decision subject to the business judgment of the directors. Id., on 23. The directors may properly decide that dividends should not be paid so that the corporation can build up a "war chest" to acquire another corporation, for purposes of growth and expansion, or for the purpose of investing its profits. Sanderson v. Bailey Brothers Corp., 29 F. 3d 250, 251-254 (2nd Cir. 2001) affirmed at 530 U.S. 62 (2001). The mere fact that the corporation has sufficient funds from which to pay a dividend does not entitle the shareholders to a dividend. ID.

The articles of incorporation may provide for a fixed dividend to one class or series of shares. Calif. Corporations Code § 8023. In such a case, the directors will be required to declare the agreed-upon dividend when legally available funds exist. Catherine Leonard, *Corporate Investment,* § 36-41 (third edition 1999). If the dividends are cumulative, any arrearages must be paid for prior years in which the corporation did not pay dividends, before any dividends can be paid to other (usually common) shareholders. California Corporations Code § 8023.

Courts are reluctant to interfere with the management of corporations, and, therefore, unless the shareholders can clearly prove bad faith or an abuse of discretion by the directors, the directors cannot be compelled to pay dividends. Leonard, id. This is yet another example of the business judgment rule, which protects directors who make business decisions in good faith. Id. As a practical matter, however, directors who fail to declare dividends when profits permit may well find themselves out of a job.

Name _____

State Your Answer – Chapter Eight
(xx points)

1. Review the Universal Citation Guide Version 2.1 at www.aallnet.org/committee/citationucg/index.html. Review Paragraph 29. In what way do the AALL Proposal and the ABA model for universal citation forms differ?

2. Access the ABA site relating to universal citation form at www.abanet.org/tech/ltrc/research/citation/home.html and review ABA Citation History.

    a. When was the first draft report on citation reform submitted?

    b. What did this report recommend?

3. Access the ABA site relating to universal citation form and review the information related to Wisconsin. What action has Wisconsin taken with regard to universal citation form?

4. Access the site of the Association of Legal Writing Directors at www.alwd.org. Select "ALWD Citation Manual" and review Chart 12.7

    a. List the divisions of your state's appellate courts.

    b. Are decisions of one court binding on other intermediate courts?

Name

Assignment for Chapter Nine
(xx points)

1. Shepardize 620 A.2d 485.

    a. Give the parallel citation.

    b. Review the abbreviations in the front of this volume. What does "NJL" stand for?

2. Locate Shepard's first reference to 179 N.W. 81.

    a. Give the parallel citation.

    b. What is the first case that follows headnote 3 of 179 N.W. 81?

    c. What is the most recent A.L.R. annotation in this volume that mentions this case?

    d. Review the abbreviations in the front of the volume. What does "CoLR" stand for?

3. Shepardize 692 N.E.2d 369.

    a. Give the parallel citations.

    b. Has this case ever been questioned? If so, give the citation.

4. Locate the first time Shepard's discusses 331 S.E.2d 846.

    a. Give the parallel citation.

    b. What negative treatment is given for this case in this volume?

5. Locate the first time Shepard's discusses 736 P.2d 161.

    a. Give the name of the case.

    b. Give the citations to the denial of *certiorari* for 736 P.2d 161.

c. What case was connected with 736 P.2d 161?

6. Use *Shepard's Southwestern Citations, Cases and Case Names* (hard cover volume, volume 2, part 6, for 2001). Locate the entries for 842 S.W.2d 704.

   a. Give the name of the case.

   b. What negative history is given for the case?

   c. Review the entries for 842 S.W.2d 580 in this volume. Was this case cited in a concurring opinion? If so, give the citation.

7. Use *Shepard's Federal Citations* (hardcover supplement, volume 2 for 2003-2004. Locate the entries for 127 F.3d 632.

   a. Give the name of this case.

   b. What Sixth Circuit case followed headnote 3 of this 1997 case?

8. Use *Shepard's Federal Citations* for the first time Shepard's mentions 831 F. Supp. 1111.

   a. Was this case affirmed? If so, give the citation to the affirming case.

   b. Retrieve the volume for the case that affirmed 831 F. Supp. 1111. Was this affirming case published?

9. Use *Shepard's United States Citations* for the first time 529 U.S. 765 is mentioned and Shepardize 529 U.S. 765 in this volume. What A.L.R. Fed. annotation discusses this case?

10. Use *Shepard's United States Citations* for the first time 468 U.S. 491 is mentioned and Shepardize 468 U.S. 91 in this volume. What was the first case to explain this case?

11. Use *Shepard's Federal Statute Citations* for 1996-2001, volume 3, hardcover supplement, and Shepardize 36 U.S.C. § 5703. Give the negative history for this statute.

12. Use *Shepard's Federal Statute Citations* for 1996-2001, volume 1, hardcover supplement, and Shepardize 15 U.S.C. § 1052(f).

    a. Which Tenth Circuit case mentions this statute?

    b. What does the delta symbol (Δ) in the citation mean?

13. Use *Shepard's Federal Statute Citations* for 2001-2003, volume 1, hardcover supplement, for the U.S. Constitution. What is the first Fourth Circuit case to discuss clause one of Article Six?

14. Use *Shepard's Federal Statute Citations* for 1996, for Tariff Schedules, Statutes at Large, and so forth.

    a. Shepardize Volume 23 of U.S. Treaties and Other International Agreements 3693. Give the history.

    b. Shepardize Rule 33 of the Rules of the Supreme Court of the United States. What Seventh Circuit case discusses this rule?

15. Use *Shepard's Acts and Cases by Popular Name (Federal and State),* 1999, Pt. 3.

    a. Give the citation to the Happy Thought Case.

    b. Give the citation to the Sickle Cell Disease Detection Act.

Name _____

State Your Answer – Chapter Nine
(xx Points)

1. Access http://lexisnexis.com/shepards and select "Shepard's Citations in Print," and then "Features" and "Specialized Citators Table." What does *Shepard's* Federal Circuit Table do?

2. Access http://lexisnexis.com/shepards and select "Features." What two report formats can you select when you Shepardize online?

3. Access http://lexisnexis.com/shepards and then "Features" and then "Product Literature." Review William L. Taylor's article about *Shepard's* and KeyCite.

    a. What is the title of this article?

    b. Review paragraph 29 of the article. What is Mr. Taylor's conclusion?

4. Access www.westlaw.com and locate information on WestCheck.com. What three tasks does WestCheck.com perform automatically?

148

Name

Assignment for Chapter Ten
(xx points)

LEGISLATIVE HISTORY

1. Use the CIS Annual Index for 2000.

    a. What public law relates to Internet false identification and prevention?

    b. Locate the CIS "Legislative History" volume for this public law.

    (i) When was it approved?

    (ii) What was its designation in the Senate?

    (iii) What days did debate occur in the House and in the Senate?

2. Use the CIS Index for 2003.

    a. For what piece of legislation did Maria C. Lehman testify?

    b. Review the CIS Abstracts for 2003. What day did Ms. Lehman testify?

    c. Who is Ms. Lehman?

3. Use *United States Code Congressional and Administrative News*.

    a. To what topic does Public Law 108-110 relate?

    b. Use Table 9 for the 108th Congress, 1st Session. Locate information relating to the Authorization of Substitute Checks (Check Clearing for the 21st Century) Act.

    (i) Give the House Bill Number.

    (ii) Give the date the bill was reported from the House.

- (iii) Give the date the bill was passed by the House.
- (iv) Give the date the bill was passed by the Senate.
- (v) Give the date the bill was approved.
- (vi) Give the Public Law Number for this legislation.

4. Review the legislative history in *United States Code Congressional and Administrative News* for the above-identified Public Law.

   a. According to House Conference Report 108-291, page 19, what is the general purpose of this bill?

   b. What volume of the *Congressional Record* includes debates relating to this legislation?

5. Review the *Congressional Record* for January 25, 2005.

   a. Who led the pledge of allegiance in the House?

   b. Which chaplain offered the prayer in the Senate?

   c. What anniversary was remembered in the Senate that day?

ADMINISTRATIVE LAW AND PRESIDENTIAL DOCUMENTS

6. Use the most recent C.F.R. Index and Finding Aids volume.

   a. What C.F.R. title and part deal with school breakfast programs?

   b. What C.F.R. title and part deal with meat inspection, specifically, disposal of diseased carcasses?

      (i) Review this provision and its subparts. What happens if a carcass is affected by brucellosis?

(ii) Must anemic carcasses be condemned?

7. Use the CCH *Blue Sky Reporter*.

   a. Use the Index. What section deals with the filing of proxy statements in annual reports?

   b. Review this section. When must copies of annual reports be furnished to the SEC?

   c. Use the Table of Cases. What section discusses *Lasker v. Burks*?

   d. Review the section discussing *Lasker v. Burks*. What proposition does the case stand for?

8. Use *Weekly Compilation of Presidential Documents*.

   a. Whose death was acknowledged on July 5, 2002?

   b. Review the "Exchange with Reporters" that occurred in Kennebunkport, Maine on July 6, 2002. Whose birthday was it that day?

INTERNATIONAL LAW

9. Use the Cumulative Index, Volume 29/30 for volumes 1601-1700 for the United Nations Treaty Series. Find the treaty that deals with friendship and delimitation of the maritime boundary between the United States and the Cook Islands. When and where was the agreement signed?

10. Use the Index for volumes 1301-1350 of the United Nations Treaty Series and find the agreement between Brazil and Argentina relating to animal health in the frontier area.

   a. Give the citations to the agreement.

   b. When did the agreement enter into force?

   c. When and where was the agreement signed?

   d. Who signed the agreement for each party?

   e. How long will the treaty remain in force?

11. Use Hackworth's *Digest of International Law*.

   a. What volume and page discuss hauling down or capture of a flag?

   b. Review this section.

      (i) Must a ship be fired upon or boarded to be captured?

      (ii) When is a vessel taken as a prize?

12. Use Whiteman's *Digest of International Law*.

    a.   What volume and page provide the definition of "shipwreck"?

    b.   Give the definition for "shipwreck."

13. Use U.S. Treaties and Other International Agreements. What is the general subject matter of 35 U.S.T. 1917 (T.I.A.S. 10769)?

14. Use *Resolutions and Decisions Adopted by the General Assembly* for the first part of the 52nd Session of the United Nations in 1997.

    a.   What is the general subject matter of the Resolution?

    b.   Was the Resolution adopted with or without a vote?

Name _____

State Your Answer – Chapter Ten
(xx points)

1. Access http://www.findlaw.com and review California Code of Civil Procedure § 1859. What does it provide regarding how statutes are to be interpreted?

2. Access the GPO Access Web site and locate the *Weekly Compilation of Presidential Documents* for August 23, 2004 (volume 40, number 34). Whose death was recognized by President Bush in a statement? Where did the individual work during World War II?

3. Review the Web site of the Internal Revenue Service. Who is the current Commissioner of the IRS and where did he receive his bachelor's degree?

4. Review title 314 of the State of Washington Administrative Code at http://www.leg.wa.gov/wac. What is the definition of "liquor"?

5. Review the Web site for the United Nations.

    a. When was the Czech Republic admitted as a member state or nation?

    b. How are peacekeepers compensated?

6. Access the site for the Municipal Code Corporation (http://www.municode.com). What does Chapter 606 (specifically section 606-3) of the Cincinnati Code of Ordinances require?

7. Access the site http:///www.uscourts.gov and locate the rules for the First Circuit. What does Local Rule 32(a) require?

Name _____

Assignment for Chapter Eleven
(xx points)

PART 1. LEXIS

1. Select "Get a Document" and "Get by Citation." Retrieve the case located at 534 U.S. 316.

    a. What is the LEXIS citation?

    b. How many pages are in the case?

    c. Select and click on the yellow triangle shown for this case. What does the yellow triangle mean? How many times has the case been distinguished by later cases?

    d. Which 2004 case from the First Circuit Court of Appeals cited this case?

2. Select "Search" at the top of the toolbar and then select the topic "Trademarks." Select "Federal and State Trademark Cases." Using natural language, locate cases relating to scandalous trademarks.

    a. Retrieve the 1993 case with the docket number 93-1464. What is the case name?

    b. Select and click on the yellow triangle shown for this case. Is there any subsequent appellate history for this case?

3. Select "Get a Document" and "Get by Citation." Enter the citation 519 U.S. 2.

    a. What is the name of this case?

    b. Select "More Like This" and then "Search." What is the first case you are directed to?

    c. Return to your original case at 519 U.S. 2. Select "Shepardize."

- (i) List the four categories of citing references that Shepard's indicates.

- (ii) Locate the 2001 law review article that mentions the case located at 519 U.S. 2. Where is the case mentioned in this law review article?

4. Select "Get a Document" and "Get by Citation." Enter 18 U.S.C.S. § 509.

   a. What does this statute relate to, generally?

   b. What Am. Jur. 2d reference are you directed to?

   c. Retrieve this Am. Jur. 2d reference. What Sixth Circuit case are you directed to for the definition of "counterfeiting"?

5. Select "Search" on the toolbar. Select "California" within "States Legal – US" and then select "Deerings California Codes Annotated." In the search box, use natural language and locate the Business and Professions Code statute relating to what paralegals' business cards should include.

   a. Give the citation for this statute.

   b. When was this statute added?

6. Select "Get a Document" and then "Party Name" and locate a United States Supreme Court case in which the plaintiff's name is A. Elliott Archer.

   a. What is the citation for this case?

   b. What is the LEXIS citation for this case?

   c. What was the disposition of this case?

7. Select "Search Advisor" on the toolbar. Explore the legal topic of "Cyberlaw." Explore "Defamation." What three legal topics are listed?

8. Select "Shepard's" on the toolbar. Using the KWIC format, Shepardize 105 N.E.2d 685.

   a. What is the name of the case you are Shepardizing?

   b. What kind of treatment does Shepard's indicate for this case by the use of its icon?

9. Select "Get a Document" and then "Docket Number." Locate the case from the United States Court of Appeals with the docket number 73-1050.

   a. What Seventh Circuit case are you directed to?

   b. Retrieve this case and then Shepardize it. What A.L.R. Fed. annotation are you directed to?

   c. Who wrote the A.L.R. Fed. annotation?

10. Select "Search" from the toolbar and then "Secondary Legal" and then "Law Reviews & Journals." Use natural language and locate U.S. articles relating to the Sarbanes-Oxley Act of 2002.

    a. What 2003 Albany Law Review article are you directed to?

    b. Review this law review article. Whom does footnote 2 quote?

11. Select "Search" and then "Find a Source." Locate the source titled "A Dictionary of Modern Legal Usage." What is a "put" in securities law?

12. Select "Search Advisor" and then "Family Law." Select "Child Custody" and then "Awards." Locate Connecticut family law cases relating to this topic. Give a brief overview of the 2005 Connecticut case in which the plaintiff's name is Denardo.

13. Select "Get a Document" and "Get by Citation." Retrieve Wash. Rev. Code § 26.10.160.

    a. What does this statute deal with, generally?

    b. Shepardize this statute. What treatment was this statute given by the United States Supreme Court?

14. Select "Search" and then "Secondary Legal" and "Restatements." Select the Restatement (Second) of Contracts (case citations). Using natural language (and date restrictions to locate cases after January 1, 2000), locate the case discussing the prison mailbox rule.

    a. What is the name of the case?

    b. According to this case, when is a prisoner's petition deemed filed?

    c. Review Restatement (Second) of Contracts § 63. What is the title of this Restatement provision?

PART II.   WESTLAW

1. At the initial Westlaw screen, in the "Find this document by citation" box, enter 568 N.W.2d 585.

    a. What is the name of this case?

    b. How many pages is the case?

    c. Select "West Reporter Image." What is the first word on page 588?

    d. Return to the case in its original format. What A.L.R. reference are you directed to?

    e. On the left side of the screen, select "KeyCite" and KeyCite this case. How many documents are listed (including this case)?

    f. Give the citation for the history of this case, namely, the appeal after remand.

2. Select "Directory" from the toolbar and select "Directories, Reference." Select *Black's Law Dictionary* (8th ed. 2004) and locate the definition for "mistrial." What is another term for mistrial?

3. Select "Directory" and continue selecting the appropriate databases to search Colorado cases. Use natural language and develop a query to locate cases from Colorado dealing with the liability of ski resorts for skiing injuries.

    a. What 1994 Colorado case are you directed to?

    b. Retrieve this case. On the left side of the screen, select "Table of Authorities." How many cases are cited in the 1994 Colorado case?

    c. Return to the case. On the left side of the screen, select "Am. Jur. Proof of Facts." What section in this article discusses the rescue duty of ski patrol?

    d. Return to the case. What KeyCite icon is displayed?

160

e. KeyCite this case. What is the subsequent history of this case?

4. Select the appropriate databases for federal statutes. Using natural language, locate the federal statute relating to copyright rights of attribution.

   a. What is the first statute you are directed to?

   b. Select this statute. Give the citation to the 1996 law review article by Geri J. Yonover that comments on the statute.

   c. Select this law review article.

      (i) How many pages is this law review article?

      (ii) What does Section IA of the article discuss?

5. Select "Directory" and the appropriate databases to use the U.S.C.A. Popular Name Index.

   a. Give the citation for the "Blue Star Mothers of America Act."

   b. Review the Act. May the corporation contribute to a political party? What section within the Act governs your answer?

6. Select "Find" on the toolbar and enter the citation 350 F.3d 810.

   a. What is the name of the case?

   b. Review headnote 3 and select or click on the KeyCite icon. What message is displayed?

c. Return to the case located at 350 F.3d 810. At the left of the screen, select "Petitions, Briefs, and Filings." Review the appellee's brief.

   (i) What does the Corporate Disclosure Statement state?

   (ii) Review the Table of Authorities in the brief. Select the *Anderson* case. Select or click on this case. What KeyCite icon is displayed?

   (iii) Select the KeyCite icon. What case declined to follow *Anderson*?

   (iv) How many green stars are displayed?

   (v) Review the KeyCite box at the left of the screen. What summary is provided for you relating to the current status of this case as good law?

7. Select "Find" and locate the case published at 898 S.W.2d 30. Select or click on the first name identified with a blue hyperlink. Identify this individual and give his or her phone number.

8. Select "Directory" and select "Administrative Material" within the "U.S. State Materials" database. Locate the attorney general opinions for California. Using natural language, search for opinions relating to smoking bans in public places.

   a. Select the opinion from October 1999. What was the question addressed to the attorney general?

   b. What answer was provided by the attorney general?

   c. What California statute was construed in the opinion?

9. Select "Directory" and "Litigation." Select "Jury Verdicts, Settlements, & Judgments" and then "Andrews Minnesota Jury Verdicts." Using natural language, retrieve information relating to medical malpractice cases decided after January 1, 2000. Select the August 2004 case relating to a teenager's death from meningitis. What was the settlement breakdown?

10. Select "KeyCite" from the toolbar and KeyCite the case located at 537 U.S. 79. Review the negative indirect history. Why didn't *Scott v. First Union Securities* follow the case located at 537 U.S. 79?

11. Select "Directory" from the toolbar and then "A.L.R." Using natural language, locate annotations relating to liability for injuries to trespassers. Select the annotation published in 70 A.L.R.3d.

    a. What Idaho case is discussed in this annotation?

    b. Review § 2 of the annotation. What is the discernable trend in this area of law?

12. Select "Find" from the toolbar and then select "Find by party name." Locate a federal case in which one of the party's names is "Grokster." When did the U.S. Supreme Court grant certiorari for this case?

13. Select "Find" from the toolbar and then select "Find this document by citation." Locate 42 U.S.C. § 1201. What does this statute relate to, generally?

14. Select "KeySearch" from the toolbar. Select "Corporations" and then "Piercing the Corporate Veil." Select Florida federal and state cases (with West headnotes) and "Search."

   a. What November 2003 case are you directed to?

   b. What key numbers appear in the yellow bands?

   c. Review the November 2003 case and KeyCite it. What occurred on January 14, 2004?

15. Select "Find" and then select "Find this document by citation" to locate the case published at 660 So. 2d 1165. Select "C" at the top of the screen. Give the name of the 1999 Florida case you are directed to.

16. Select "Find" and then "Find a case by party name." How many federal cases are there in which a party's name is "Grainer"?

17. Select "Directory" and then A.L.R. Using natural language, locate an annotation in A.L.R.4th that relates to inhalation of asbestos (and product liability).

   a. Give the citation to the annotation.

   b. Who is the author of the annotation?

   c. What section of the annotation discusses sophisticated users of asbestos products?

18. Select "Find" and then select "Find this document by citation" to locate the document designated as 2003 WL 23004289. What is this document?

_____
Name

State Your Answer – Chapter Eleven
(xx points)

1. Access LEXIS's Directory of Online Sources at http://web.nexis.com/sources. Use the field titled "Geography" and select your state. Determine LEXIS's coverage for your state's attorney general opinions.

2. Access Westlaw's Database Directory at http://directory.westlaw.com/?tf=90&tc=11.

    a. Give the appropriate database identifier for cases from your state's courts.

    b. Give the appropriate database identifier for annotated statutes from your state.

    c. Give the appropriate database identifier for the George Mason Law Review.

Name

Assignment for Chapter Twelve
(xx points)

1. Access THOMAS.

    a. Select "Public Laws" and select for the 108th Congress. What is the purpose of P.L. 108-126?

    b. Review the text of this law. When was it approved?

2. Return to THOMAS and locate information relating to the House Agriculture Committee.

    a. When was the committee created?

    b. How many subcommittees does the Committee include?

3. Return to THOMAS and access the Senate Directory. Obtain information relating to Senator DeWine from Ohio.

    a. When was Senator DeWine born?

    b. How many children does Senator DeWine have?

    c. When was Senator DeWine first elected to the Senate?

4. Return to THOMAS and select "Historical Documents."

    a. Select the Declaration of Independence. When was it drafted?

    b. Select the Federalist Papers. Who is the author of the General Introduction? Who is the author of the 41st paper relating to powers conferred by the Constitution?

5. Access the FirstGov site and select "A-Z Agency Index." Select the American Battle Monument Commission and review information relating to the cemetery in Normandy, France. How many graves of American military dead are in the cemetery?

6. Return to the A-Z Agency Index for FirstGov. Select the Patent and Trademark Office.

    a. Select "Trademarks" and conduct a "basic user search" to locate the trademark "You Deserve a Break Today." When was this mark registered?

    b. Select "Patents" and search for the following patent: No. 6,004,596. What is the invention patented?

    c. For the above patent, select "Images." What is shown on the screen?

7. Access the site MegaLaw and select "Entertainment law." Select ASCAP and then select "ACE Title Search." By selecting "writer," locate the songs written by Billy Joel.

    a. How many songs are identified?

    b. Select "Shameless." Who are identified as performers of the song?

8. Access the site www.uscourts.gov and select information relating to the U.S. Bankruptcy Courts. Review "Bankruptcy Basics." What is a Chapter 7 bankruptcy?

9. Return to www.uscourts.gov and identify the address of the U.S. District Court for the Western District of Texas (San Antonio division).

10. Access the site for the U.S. Supreme Court (www.supremecourtus.gov) and select "Public Information." Review the Chief Justice's Year-End Report on the Federal Judiciary for 2004.

   a. Review Section II. Which circuits have not had any new judgeships for twenty years?

   b. Review Section IV. Why was there an eleven per cent increase in civil filings?

11. Access FindLaw and select for federal laws. In the appropriate search boxes, search for 35 U.S.C. § 101. What does this statute provide?

12. Return to FindLaw and select for U.S. Supreme Court cases.

   a. In the citation search box, search for 525 U.S. 121. What is the defendant's name?

   b. In the party name search box, enter "Bush" and search for *Bush v. Gore*. Who delivered the opinion of the Court? Which Justices dissented?

13. Access the site for GPO Access. Select the *Federal Register*, and browse the table of contents for 2004. Select the *Federal Register* table of contents for Wednesday, December 29, 2004. Review the material for the Education Department.

    a. Generally, what proposed rule is set forth?

    b. Review the proposed rule. When must comments be received by the Department of Education on this proposed rule?

Name _____

State Your Answer – Chapter Twelve
(xx points)

1. Access either FindLaw or MegaLaw. How many witnesses are needed in your state when a will is executed?

2. Access the site for the National Association for Secretaries of State (http://www.nass.org). Who is the secretary of state for your state?

3. Access the site Hoover's at http://www.hoovers.com. Locate information for Delta Air Lines, Inc.

    a. What is the ticker symbol for Delta?

    b. What is the company's phone number?

    c. When is the company's fiscal year-end?

    d. Who are the company's top competitors?

4. Access the site FirstGov. Select "State Government" and then "State Legislatures." Locate your state's constitution. What is the title of Article 1 of your state's constitution?

5. Access Google. Enter "rcw 4.16.005." What are you referred to? What does this section provide?

6. Use Google and locate the home page for Oklahoma Association of Wine Producers.

    a. Who established the first successful winery in Indian Territory?

    b. What was the value of wines in 1996?

    c. Review the copyright notice at the end of the site. What message are you given?

_____
Name

State Your Answer – Chapter Thirteen
(xx points)

1. Access the site http://www.ll.georgetown.edu/lib/guides/cost.html. What is the last tip provided to help keep research costs under control?

2. Access the "Research Steps Tutorial" at the site http://www.lawschool.cornell.edu/lawlibrary/Finding_the_Law. What is the beginning stage of legal research?

3. Access the site http://www.lectlaw.com/study.html and review "Ten Easy Steps to Legal Research." What is the final step?

Name

Assignment for Chapter Fourteen
(xx points)

GRAMMAR

SELECT THE CORRECT WORD.

1. The deposition transcript was received by Jill and her/she.

2. For who/whom did the witness testify?

3. The SEC has released its/it's/its' findings.

4. Jack and him/he attended the hearing.

5. Someone has left his-her/their briefcase in the courtroom.

6. The company held it's/its annual meeting today.

7. The subpoena must be served on Tom, James, and he/him.

8. The committee, together with the members, have/has issued the report.

9. Each of the exhibits are/is indexed in the closing binder.

10. Only one of the documents for the hearings have/has been summarized.

SPELLING

SELECT THE CORRECT SPELLING.

1. admissible   admissable

2. decedant   decedent

3. dependant   dependent

4. privilege   privelege

5. occasion   occassion

6. organization   organisation

7.	judgement	judgment
8.	inadvertant	inadvertent
9.	interrogatories	interogatories
10.	the foregoing section	the forgoing section

PUNCTUATION

CORRECTLY PUNCTUATE THE FOLLOWING SENTENCES.

1. Both judges chambers were recently redecorated.

2. The motion was heard on January 3, 2005 and resulted in a change of venue.

3. Following are various remedies that may be granted by a court; compensatory damages, punitive damages and equitable relief.

4. Judge Harris opinion was lengthy.

5. The transcript however was not included with the other documents.

6. Alice Bowen the former senator, attended the meeting.

7. The jurys decision was unanimous.

8. The first witness was late. Which made the judge angry.

9. There were two omissions in the agreement they were both in paragraph two.

10. He is an extremely diligent paralegal and he is always prepared to help.

State Your Answer – Chapter Fourteen
(xx points)

1. Access the Web site of the U.S. Government Printing Office Style Manual.

   a. Review Rule 3 relating to capitalization and either correct the following or indicate if they are correct.

   - I live near the lake. Its name is lake Deepcreek.
   - I lived in the west. Travel in a westerly direction.
   - I live in San Diego County. The County is large.

   b. Review Rule 8 relating to punctuation and either correct the following or indicate if they are correct.

   - Your boss's memo is complete.
   - The mens' cars were parked outside.
   - Jefferson Davis' home was in Richmond.
   - The trial began in June, 2004.
   - Send me the April 15, 2005 report.
   - She was a tense, angry witness.

2. Access http://www.bartleby.com and review *The Elements of Style*.

   a. Review Section II.1 and use the correct punctuation to make the following expressions possessives: the friend of Charles, the poems of Burns, and the malice of the witch.

   b. Review Section II.2 and punctuate the following sentence: He opened the letter read it and made a note of its contents.

175

Name _____

Assignment for Chapter Fifteen
(xx points)

PRECISION

SELECT THE CORRECT WORD IN THE FOLLOWING SENTENCES.

1. The effect/affect of the expert's testimony was negligible.

2. The company's principle/principal office is in Atlanta.

3. She agreed to the terms of the parenting agreement during our oral/verbal telephone conversation.

4. The settlement was entered into between/among all four litigants.

5. The jury found him liable for/guilty of malpractice.

6. All attorneys must insure/ensure their clients are prepared for their depositions.

7. The jury was affected/effected by Ms. Lane's testimony.

8. Tina prepared the only memoranda/memorandum this week.

9. Beside/Besides the bailiff, the marshal also performed security checks in the courtroom.

10. "It's the principal/principle of the thing," the client told her attorney.

CLARITY

REPHRASE EACH OF THE FOLLOWING TO PRODUCE A CLEARER SENTENCE.

1. The contract was signed on April 4. The parties' agreement was later amended in May.

2. We are not precluded from claiming that Dr. Smith failed to adhere to a not unreasonable standard of care.

3. We do not deny that scandalous trademarks are unprotectable under the U.S. Trademark Act.

4. The witness arrived early for her deposition. The deponent later tired in the afternoon.

5. We cannot fail to allege that the defendant refused to repair the leased premises.

6. Although the seller paid taxes on the property, the vendor failed to obtain title insurance for the parcel.

7. The defendant's motorcycle collided with the pedestrian. The motor vehicle was then sold for scrap metal.

8. We cannot forget to ensure that Ms. Smith is not unprepared for trial.

9. Mr. Phillips told Mr. Ruiz that he must attend the settlement conference.

10. The bank released the financial statements on Friday. This was a violation of its obligations to maintain the records in confidence.

READABILITY

REWRITE THE FOLLOWING SENTENCES TO MAKE THEM MORE READABLE BY USING THE ACTIVE VOICE.

1. A decision was announced by the Supreme Court that affected all claims brought under the new legislation.

2. The election held by the corporation resulted in approval of the directors nominated by the committee.

3. An agreement to settle the case was approved by the judge.

4. A confidentiality agreement was signed by all of the company's employees.

5. The transcript was prepared by the court reporter after a hearing was held by the judge.

REWRITE THE FOLLOWING SENTENCES TO MAKE THEM MORE READABLE BY USING PARALLEL STRUCTURE.

1. The critical characteristics of effective paralegals are attention to detail, organizational skills, and being flexible.

2. Indexing documents and preparation of letters to clients were two of Mary's job duties.

3. The settlement agreement required the defendant to pay $50,000, sign a confidentiality agreement, and refraining from making any further statements to the media.

4. The clients were instructed to sign the promissory note, depositing the money into the escrow account, and file a copy of the deed of trust with the clerk's office.

5. Careful proofreading and making edits to documents is key to ensuring their accuracy.

6. There are two steps to closing the file: first, returning the original documents to the client; and secondly, preparing the summary of the file contents.

REWRITE THE FOLLOWING SENTENCES TO MAKE THEM MORE READABLE BY ELIMINATING JARGON.

1. Until such time as they execute the agreement, the parties have agreed and consented to cease and desist from any and all activities related to discovery in the instant case at bar.

2. In the event that the document evidences fraud or deceit in its inception or making, the plaintiff shall be required to apprise the defendant antecedent to commencing litigation.

3. The first parcel of land is contiguous and adjacent to the second.

4. At her deposition, the defendant will be required to elucidate her reason for failing and refusing to consummate the purchase transaction relating to the real estate in question.

5. In reference to your lease, we opine that the remainder of the rent that is due and owing must be paid to the landlord.

Name _____

State Your Answer – Chapter Fifteen
(xx points)

1. Review the handout *Writing User-Friendly Documents* at the Plain Language Web site at http://www.plainlanguage.gov. Review page 19. What is a "noun sandwich" and how can it be avoided?

2. Review the SEC's guidance document *Plain English Handbook* at http://www.sec.gov. Review Chapter 6. What are the most common writing problems that the SEC has encountered?

3. Access Purdue University's Online Writing Lab at http://owl.english.purdue.edu. Review the handout entitled "Parallel Structure."

    a. What is the third rule that the Lab recommends to avoid problems with parallel structure?

    b. What proofreading strategies are recommended to avoid problems with parallel structure?

4. Access Professor Eugene Volokh's site at http://www1.law.ucla.edu/~volokh/legalese.htm. What substitutions are recommended for the following terms of legalese: "evince," "negatively affect," and "substantiate"?

5. Access the site http://www.ccc.commnet.edu/grammar and review the information on Writer's Block. What is the worst part of the writing experience for many writers?

Name _____

Assignment for Chapter Sixteen
(xx points)

You have been given the following fact pattern by Alison Keane, one of the senior partners in your law firm.

The firm represents Outdoor Artists, Inc., a corporation formed in our state and which is engaged in landscape design in our city, near the state border. The president of the corporation is Edward Davis. For several years the corporation provided services only in our state. During the past year, however, because the city is so close to the state border, the corporation has also been providing services in the adjacent state. Specifically, the corporation opened a bank account in the adjacent state and performed landscaping services for five different customers in the adjacent state. One customer, Leo Mahony, has refused to pay for the services and the client wants to sue Mr. Mahony to recover the money owed. Another customer, Jill Lopez, has sued the client, alleging that the client damaged her drainage system when it performed landscaping services for her.

Ms. Keane is concerned because the client has not qualified to transact business as a foreign corporation in the adjacent state (as required by state statute) and would like you to prepare an opinion letter (for her signature) to the client regarding the possible effects of the client's failure to qualify to transact business. By way of background, the Model Business Corporation Act provides that before a corporation may transact business in a state other than the state of its incorporation, it must qualify to transact business as a foreign corporation, a fairly simple process involving filing a form and asking the foreign state's permission to conduct business in its borders. Our state has adopted the Act in its entirety and the Act is available on the American Bar Association's Web site at http://www.abanet.org. Assume there are no cases interpreting the applicable provisions of the Act.

_____
                                                              Name

State Your Answer – Chapter Sixteen
(xx points)

1. Access the site
   http://writing.colostate.edu/references/documents/bletter/index.cfm.

   a. Review the section relating to formatting letters. How should the complementary close be punctuated?

   b. Review the section called "Effective Letter-Writing Principles." Why do many executives prefer written documents to other forms of communication?

2. Access the site http://www.business-letter-writing.com. Review the checklist for writing business letters. What four tips are given?

Name _____

State Your Answer – Chapter Seventeen
(xx points)

1. Access the site http://www.lawnerds.com/guide/irac.html.

   a. What is the key to issue spotting?

   b. Review the section called "Conclusion." What is a common mistake made by many students in conclusions?

2. Access the site http://www.ccc.commnet.edu/grammar. Review the information relating to thesis statements. Give the definition of a thesis statement.

3. Access the site http://www.yourlawprof.com/21f/law34/legalmemonotes.htm. What are the three functions of a legal memorandum?

Court Brief Exercise for Chapter Eighteen

To: Paralegal

From: Daniel L. Lodge, Partner

Our client, Marisa Bailey, is an 18-year old high school senior who attends James River High School ("James River"). James River is operated by Rio Grande Unified School District (the "District"), a school district that operates elementary, middle, and secondary schools in this district. In planning its graduation ceremony and program, James River notified parents of the graduating seniors that student-led and student-initiated nondenominational prayers would be offered at the graduation. School officials at James River will review any prayers before they are offered at the ceremony. Attendance at graduation is voluntary.

Ms. Bailey has sued the District on the basis that such prayers violate the First Amendment's prohibition against laws relating to establishment of religion. We intend to move for summary judgment on behalf of Ms. Bailey. Please prepare a brief (or memorandum of law) in support of a motion for summary judgment that will persuade the United States District Court for the Anywhere District that any such prayers offered at the school graduation would violate the First Amendment to the U.S. Constitution.

Court rules impose a ten-page limit on all briefs. In addition, court rules require that the brief be typewritten, double spaced, and that current *Bluebook* or *ALWD* citation format be followed.

Name

Assignment for Chapter Eighteen
(xx points)

You have been asked to prepare the table of authorities for an appellate brief to be filed in the United States District Court. There are no special rules for citation form. You should use the rules set forth in the current edition of the *Bluebook* or *ALWD*. Do not worry about the page numbers. The following citations will appear in the brief.

Daly v. O'Brien, 109 F.3d 111, 121 (Eighth Circuit 2000)

15 U.S.C. § 1051(a)

Forrest v. Sullivan Insurance Indemnity Company, 520 U.S. 16, 230 S. Ct. 790,

    189 L. Ed. 2d 42 (2001)

Lehman v. Moore, 909 F.2d 550 (3rd Cir. 1998)

15 U.S.C. § 1051(b)

Nelson v. Lyons, 15 F. Supp. 3d (District Court New Jersey 2001)

DeLansing v. Kirk, 525 U.S. 909 (2002)

State v. Reynolds, 789 N.E.2d 199 (N.Y. 1989)

In re Walsh, 799 N.E. 2d 42, 44 (New York 1991)

New York Domestic Relations Code Section 445

42 U.S.C. Section 2242

Gregory v. Young, 121 F.3d 889 (8th Circ. 2002)

New York Commerce Code § 330

187

                                                                    _____
                                                                         Name

                    State Your Answer – Chapter Eighteen
                                  (xx points)

1.   Use MegaLaw (http://www.megalaw.com) to access the local rules for the First
     Circuit Court of Appeals. Review Rule 32. What is the maximum length for a
     reply brief?

2.   Access the site http://www.ualr.edu/~cmbarger. Select "Appellate Resources"
     and then "Persuasive Strategies for Appellate Brief-Writing." What is the first
     strategy?

3.   Access the site http://www.appellate.net/briefs. Review the amicus curiae brief
     filed in *Anderson v. General Motors Corp*. What is the argument heading for
     Argument I?

4.   Access MegaLaw. What cases can be found for your state?

Name

Assignment for Chapter Nineteen
(xx points)

Carefully proofread the following passage and make the necessary corrections.

Our client, Jack Patterson is a convicted sex offendor who was convicted of incest. Patterson pled guilty and was given a ten year sentence to be followed by three years' of supervised probation. As part of his setnece, the court barred Patterson from using a computer or any other device with Internet capabilities, even in the performance of his job. The judge who imposed the sentence stated that the risk of Pattersen reoffending is to great to allow him to have any Internet access. The court noted that Pattersen could use the internet to lure young victims and engage in porngraphy.

There have been a number of cases in this circuit and other circuit tht have discussed this issue. Most of those cases have held that restrictions on computer and internet use are overly braod and are unreasaonble if they are not related to the convicts crime. In the pesent case, Patterson did not use the Internet to engage in the criminal act of incest. Its been held that it makes no more sense to deny an offender Internet access than to bar a wire fraud perpetrator access to their telephone.

Patterson's bakground in information technology and to provide for himself he will need Internet access upon his release from prison. Patterson has asked us to research the following two issues: do they have the right to bar him from using the Internet, may the bar be permanant, and whether the sentence is reasonably related to his crime.

Please prepare a written memoranda for my by Friday morning a.m.

Name

State Your Answer – Chapter Nineteen
(xx points)

1. Access the site http://www.ucc.vt.edu/stdysk/proofing.html.

    a. Why does it help to read aloud?

    b. How many times do professional editors proofread a document?

2. Review the Federal Rule of Appellate Procedure 32 for the Ninth Circuit at http://www.ca9.uscourts.gov.

    a. What type styles may be used in documents?

    b. What word counts are imposed for principal briefs?

3. Review the proofreading marks found at http://www.prenhall.com/author_guide/proofing.html.

    a. What does the mark "flush" mean?

    b. What does the mark "Eq #" mean?

**Answer Keys
For
Library Assignments and State Your Answers**

Note to Instructors: It is possible that some answers have changed since the date of publication of this Instructors' Manual. For example, some pocket part updates may affect some answers in the library assignments, and some of the answers in the "State Your Answers" sections may have changed, such as those relating to various state officials. The appropriate website addresses are given for the "State Your Answer" assignments. Thus, instructors may easily update those answers.

Name
Assignment for Chapter One
(xx points)

1.   a.   Give the name of the case located at 531 U.S. 70 (2000).

   Bush v. Palm Beach County Canvassing Board

   b.   Who argued the case for the Petitioner? **Theodore B. Olson**

2.   a.   Give the name of the case located at 447 U.S. 303 (1980).

   Diamond v. Chakrabarty

   b.   Who delivered the opinion of the Court? **Chief Justice Burger**

   c.   Who dissented? **Justice Brennan (joined by Justices White, Marshall,**

   and Powell)

3.   a.   Give the name of the case at 502 U.S. 301 (1992).

   Molzoff v. United States

   b.   Give the date the case was argued. **November 4, 1991**

   c.   Give the date the case was decided. **January 14, 1992**

   d.   Locate a case in this volume in which the defendant's name is *Bryant* and give the name of the case. ***Hunter v. Bryant***

   e.   Give the citation for the *Bryant* case. **502 U.S. 224 (1991)**

   f.   What part did Justice Thomas take in the *Bryant* case? **No part**

(Justice Thomas took no part in the consideration of decision of this case.)

Name _____

State Your Answer – Chapter One
(xx points)

1. Use Table T.1 of the *Bluebook* or access http://www.ncsconline.org (the website for the National Center for State Courts) and locate and access your state's judicial website. Who is the current chief justice or senior judge of your state's highest court?

    Answers can be accessed through:
    http://www.ncsconline.org/D_KIS/info_court_web_sites.html#State
    California: Chief Justice Ronald M. George
    Florida: Chief Justice Barbara J. Pariente
    New York: Chief Judge Judith S. Kaye
    Texas: Chief Justice Thomas R. Phillips

2. Access the site for the American Association for Law Libraries and identify the state, court, or county law libraries in your state or nearest locality.

    Answers are located at:
    http://www.aallnet.org/sis/sccll/membership/libraries.htm
    California: Eleven law libraries identified
    Florida: Four law libraries identified
    New York: Six law libraries identified (including four in NYC)
    Texas: Seven law libraries identified

3. Access the site for GPO Access and identify at least one federal depository library for your state or nearest locality.

    Answers are located at:
    http://www.gpoaccess.gov/libraries.html

4. Access Cornell Law School's Legal Information Institute at http://www.cornell.edu. Select "Lexicon" and provide the definition for *stare decisis*.

    "Latin for "to stand by things decided." Stare decisis is essentially the doctrine of precedent. Courts cite to stare decisis when an issue has been previously brought to the court and a ruling already issued. Generally, courts will adhere to the previous ruling, though this is not universally true."

Name _____

Assignment for Chapter Two
(xx points)

1.   a.   Give the name of the case located at 531 U.S. 57 (2000).

   Eastern Associated Coal v. United Mine Workers of America

   b.   Give the holding of the case. **Affirmed**

   c.   During the period of time covered by the cases in the volume, which United States Supreme Court Justice was assigned or allotted to the Tenth Circuit?   **Justice Stephen Breyer**

   d.   Locate a case in this volume in which the plaintiff's name is *Buckman Co.*

        (i)   Give the full name and citation of this case.

   ***Buckman Co. v. Plaintiff's Legal Counsel*, 531 U.S. 341 (2001)**

        (ii)   Who was the United States Attorney General at the time this case was decided?   **U.S. Attorney General was John Ashcroft who took office on 2/1/01. [Note: The previous U.S. Attorney General was Janet Reno, who resigned on 1/20/01. This case was decided on 2/21/01.]**

2.   a.   Locate a case in volume 502 of the *U.S. Reports* in which the plaintiff's name is *Byers* and give the name and citation of this case.

   ***Byers v. Armontrout*, 502 U.S. 1007 (1991)**

   b.   Give the result reached in this case.   **Certiorari was denied.**

3.   To which circuits are the following states assigned?

        a.   Utah   **Tenth Circuit**
        b.   Connecticut   **Second Circuit**
        c.   Missouri   **Eighth Circuit**

4.   a.   Give the name of the case located at 154 F.3d 161 (4th Cir. 1998).

   Pope v. Hunt **(students may use another plaintiff's name and refer to this as *Shaw v. Hunt*)**

   b.   Which judge issued the opinion of the court? **Senior Judge Campbell**

5. a. Give the name of the case located at 33 F. Supp. 2d 78.

Somes v. United Airlines Inc.

b. Which of the United States District Courts decided this case? **D. Mass.**

c. Who represented the defendant in this case? **Peter J. Black, Meehan, Boyle & Cohen, P.C., Boston, MA.**

Name _____

State Your Answer – Chapter Two
(xx points)

1. Access the site http://www.uscourts.gov and review the map of federal circuits and districts.

   a. In which circuit is your state located?

   b. In which district court would you file a complaint for age discrimination?

   Answers are located at:
   http://www.uscourts.gov/images/CircuitMap.pdf
   California: Ninth Circuit (C.D., E.D., N.D., S.D.)
   Florida: Eleventh Circuit (M.D., N.D., S.D.)
   New York: Second Circuit (E.D., N.D., S.D., W.D.)
   Texas: Fifth Circuit (E.D., N.D., S.D., W.D.)

2. Access the site for the National Center for State Courts at http://ncsconline.org and locate the "State Court Structure Charts."

   a. How many justices sit on your state's highest court?

   b. What are the names of your state's courts?

   Answers can be located by inserting the terms "State Court Structure Charts" into the search box provided on the left side of the homepage for this site. Alternatively, answers can be located by accessing: http://www.ncsconline.org/D_Research/csp/2003_Files/ 2003_SCCS.html and then selecting "State Court Structure Charts.

   California: 7 Justices. Courts are Supreme Court, Courts of Appeal, and Superior Courts
   Florida: 7 Justices. Courts are Supreme Court (and District Court of Appeals), Circuit Courts, and County Courts (Two appellate courts and two trial courts)
   New York: 7 Justices. New York's court structure is likely the most complex in the nation. Briefly, its major divisions consist of the Court of Appeals, the Appellate Divisions and Terms of the Supreme Court, the Supreme Court, and the Court of Claims.
   Texas: 9 Justices. Its courts are the Supreme Court (and the Supreme Court of Criminal Appeals), the Courts of Appeals, the District Courts, the County level courts, and the Municipal Courts.

3. Within the site for the National Center for State Courts, select "Court Statistics Project" and then locate "State Court Caseload Statistics." Review Table 2. How many total cases (including both mandatory and discretionary petitions) were filed in your state's highest court?

Answers can be located by accessing:
http://www.ncsconline.org/D_Research/csp/2003_Files/
2003_SCCS.html (and then selecting Table 2).
As of 2003:   **California:**   **8,917**
                 Florida: **2,777**
                 New York: **4,278**
                 Texas: **1,301**

Name

Assignment for Chapter Three
(xx points)

1. What title of the United States Code relates to Shipping? **Title 46**

2. Use U.S.C.A. and cite the title and section that govern the following:

    a. Research relating to lupus. **42 U.S.C.A. § 285d-6a**

    b. Definitions of African elephants. **16 U.S.C.A. § 4244**

3. Use either U.S.C.A. or U.S.C.S. and cite the title and section that govern the following:

    a. Smallpox vaccines and vaccinations. **42 U.S.C.A. or U.S.C.S. § 300hh-12**
    b. Beer as being nonmailable. **18 U.S.C.A. or U.S.C.S. § 1716**

4. Use the Popular Name tables as directed and cite the title and section for the following:

    a. Use U.S.C.A. and give the citation for the short title of the Sarbanes-Oxley Act of 2002. **15 U.S.C.A. § 7201note**

    b. Use U.S.C.A. and give the citation for Jennifer's Law.
    42 U.S.C.A. § 14661 note and 42 U.S.C.A. §§ 14661-14664

    c. Use either U.S.C.A. or U.S.C.S. and give the citation for the Boggs Act.
    21 U.S.C.A. or U.S.C.S. § 174

    d. Use either U.S.C.A. or U.S.C.S. and give the citation for the Muhammad Ali Boxing Reform Act.
    **15 U.S.C.A. §§ 6301 note, 6307a to 6307h, 6308 to 6313;
    or 15 U.S.C.S. § 6301 nt.**

5. Use either U.S.C.A. or U.S.C.S. and describe the counseling available for veterans who are victims of sexual trauma.

> **38 U.S.C.A. or U.S.C.S. § 1720D provides that through December 31, 2004, the Secretary should operate a program providing counseling and care to veterans who the Secretary determines require such to overcome psychological trauma which resulted from a physical assault of a sexual nature, battery of a sexual nature, or sexual harassment while the veteran was on active duty.**

6. Use the U.S.C.A. volumes for the Constitution. Answer the following questions and cite the best case to support your answer. Give case names only.

   a. Under the First Amendment (Freedom of Religion), does requiring mandatory chapel attendance for cadets and midshipmen at federal military academies violate the Establishment Clause? **Yes.** *Anderson v. Laird*

   b. Under the Eighth Amendment, is denial of warm food cruel and unusual punishment? **No.** *McCoy v. Goord* **(found in supplement) or** *Pinkston v. Bensinger* **(found in regular hardbound volume)**

7. Use U.S.C.A. Give an answer to the question and cite the best case to support your answer. Give case name only.

   a. Under 18 U.S.C.A. § 1302, is "keno" a "lottery" within the meaning of internal revenue laws? **No.** *Homes v. Bradshaw*

   b. What encyclopedia reference are you directed to in order to better understand this statute? **Postal Service & Offenses against Postal Laws C.J.S. § 23**

8. Use U.S.C.S. Answer the following questions and cite the best case to support your answer. Give case names only.

   a. Under 29 U.S.C.S. § 152, are interns, residents, and fellows employed by medical centers "employees"? **Yes.** *Boston Medical Center Corp.*

   b. Under 15 U.S.C.S. § 1052, may a trademark including the letters "U.S." prominently displayed be registered as a trademark? **No.** *Re United States Rubber Company*

9. Use *U.S. Statutes at Large*.

    a. What is the short title of Public Law 107-296? **Homeland Security Act of 2002**

    b. Give the citation for this law in *U.S. Statutes at Large*. **116 Stat. 2135**

    c. What was its designation in the House of Representatives? **HR 5005**

10. Use *U.S. Statutes at Large*.

    a. For whose relief was Private Law 106-14 enacted? **Wei Jinsheng**

    b. What was the purpose of Private Law 106-5?

        To determine the vessel M/V Mist Cove to be less than 100 gross tons, as measured under Chapter 145 of title 46, U.S. Code (so that the vessel would be determined to be a "small passenger vessel")

Name_____

State Your Answer – Chapter Three
(xx points)

1. Access one of the Internet sites for the United States Senate and identify your state's two senators.

   Answers may be obtained at a variety of sites, including THOMAS at http://thomas.loc.gov/.
   California: Barbara Boxer and Dianne Feinstein
   Florida: Bob Graham and Bill Nelson
   New York: Hillary Clinton and Charles Schumer
   Texas: John Cornyn and Kay Hutchison

2. Access the National Conference on State Legislatures (www.ncsonline.org) and select the appropriate topics and links.

   a. Identify the two legislative bodies in your state (one in Nebraska).

      Answers may be located at http://www.ncsl.org/public/leglinks.cfm.
      California: Assembly and Senate
      Florida: House of Representatives and Senate
      New York: Assembly and Senate
      Texas: House of Representatives and Senate

   b. Determine whether your state imposes term limits on its legislative representatives. If it does, describe those limits.

      Answers may be located at http://www.ncsl.org/programs/legman/about/states.htm.
      As of mid-2003, only 15 states had term limits (Arizona, Arkansas, California, Colorado, Florida, Louisiana, Maine, Michigan, Missouri, Montana, Nebraska, Nevada, Ohio, Oklahoma, and South Dakota).
      California: Limits terms in the Assembly and in the Senate to 8 years.
      Florida: Limits terms in the House and in the Senate to 8 years.

3. Use FindLaw (http://www.findlaw.com) to link to your state's statutes. Review the business organizations or corporations statutes for your state and give your state's definition of the term "corporation."

    California: "Corporation", unless otherwise expressly provided, refers only to a corporation organized under this division or a corporation subject to this division under the provisions of subdivision (a) of Section 102. Cal. Corp. Code § 162.

    Florida: "Corporation" or "domestic corporation" means a corporation for profit, which is not a foreign corporation, incorporated under or subject to the provisions of this act. Fla. Stat. Ann. § 607.01401

    New York: "Corporation" or "domestic corporation" means a corporation for profit formed under this chapter, or existing on its effective date and theretofore formed under any other general statute or by any special act of this state for a purpose or purposes for which a corporation may be formed under this chapter, other than a corporation which may be formed under the cooperative corporations law. New York Bus. Corp. Law § 102 (a)(4).

    Texas: "Corporation" or "domestic corporation" means a corporation for profit subject to the provisions of this Act, except a foreign corporation. Tex. Bus. Corp. Act art. 1.02(A)(11).

4. Use either the *Bluebook* or *ALWD* and determine which publisher publishes the compiled statutes in your state. Note that some states publish only officially and no publisher will be identified.
Answers can be located in Table T.1 of the *Bluebook* or Appendix 1 of *ALWD*.

    California: Statutes are published by both West and Deering
    Florida: Statutes are published officially and by West. The *Bluebook* (but not *ALWD*) also indicates they are published by LexisNexis.
    New York: Statutes are published by both McKinney and Gould (and by LexisNexis in a set called "Consolidated"0
    Texas: Statutes are published by Vernon

Sample Case Brief for Chapter Four
[Note that other forms and styles are also acceptable]

PepsiCo v. Redmond, 54 F.3d 1262 (7th Cir. 1995)

PROCEDURAL HISTORY

Plaintiff PepsiCo, Inc. ("PepsiCo") sought a preliminary injunction against defendant Redmond and the Quaker Oats Company ("Quaker") to prevent defendant Redmond, a former PepsiCo employee, from permanently divulging PepsiCo trade secrets to defendant Quaker, Redmond's new employer, and assuming certain duties with Quaker for approximately five months. The District Court for the Northern District of Illinois granted the injunction, the defendants appealed, and this court affirmed.

FACTS

Redmond worked for PepsiCo in a relatively high-level position that gave him access to company inside information and trade secrets, especially relating to PepsiCo's sports drink products. Like other managers, Redmond had signed a confidentiality agreement with PepsiCo agreeing not to disclose PepsiCo's confidential information to others. Redmond accepted a job with Quaker in its sports drink division as its chief operating officer but was less than candid with PepsiCo when he pursued and then accepted his new job. PepsiCo then sought to enjoin him from assuming his duties and Quaker and divulging PepsiCo confidential information to his new employer.

ISSUES

May a court enjoin the actual or threatened misappropriation of trade secrets?

ANSWER

Yes. If a plaintiff can demonstrate that a party's new employment will inevitably lead him to rely on the plaintiff's trade secrets, a court may enjoin such inevitable disclosure.

REASONING

Redmond possessed extensive and intimate knowledge about PepsiCo's goals, marketing, and distribution for its sports drink market. It is inevitable that Redmond would rely on PepsiCo's trade secrets in his new job at Quaker. Although workers should not be prevented from pursuing their livelihoods when they leave their jobs, in this case, unless Redmond possessed an uncanny ability to compartmentalize information, he would necessarily rely on his significant knowledge of PepsiCo's trade secrets in his new job. These trade secrets would provide a substantial advantage to Quaker, which would be able to anticipate PepsiCo's marketing moves. In view of the demonstrated inevitability that Redmond would rely on PepsiCo's trade secrets in his new job (which would cause him to breach his confidentiality agreement) and the district court's determination that Redmond's previous lack of candor caused the court to doubt that Redmond would refrain from disclosing the secrets in his new position, the district court correctly decided that PepsiCo had demonstrated a likelihood of success on its claim of trade secret misappropriation, and therefore its granting of an injunction was appropriate. Moreover, the scope of the injunction relating to Redmond's duties with Quaker, which was limited in its length and as to certain duties only, extended no further than necessary and was thus within the district court's discretion.

HOLDING

The court affirmed the holding of the district court.

Name

Assignment for Chapter Four
(xx points)

1. Give the name of the case located at 667 N.W.2d 467 (Minn. Ct. App. 2003) and state what the case involves.

    ***In the Matter of the Welfare of M.A.K.* involves an in-school interview between police and a juvenile and the necessity of Miranda warnings.**

2. Use 39 P.3d. What case in this volume construes the meaning of "dwelling"?

    State v. Kautz

3. Give the author of the opinion for the case located at 540 U.S. 544 (2004).

    No author is identified in this per curiam opinion.

4. Use 710 N.E.2d. What case in this volume construes Mass. Gen. Laws ch. 272, § 17?

    ***Commonwealth v. Smith*, 710 N.E.2d 1003**

5. Locate the case at 846 A.2d 318 (D.C. 2004).

    a. Give the name of the case. ***Chang v. Institute for Public-Private Partnerships, Inc.***

    b. What does headnote 7 discuss?

    It discusses the District of Columbia Family and Medical Leave Act, which permits a cause of action for termination in retaliation for taking protected leave.

6. What is the name of the case located at 163 F.3d 238 (5th Cir. 1998)?

    United States v. $9,041,598.68

7. What is the name of the case located at 308 F. Supp. 798 (S.D.N.Y. 1970)?

   Ruggiero v. Rederiet for M/S Marion

8. What is the name of the case located at 679 F. Supp. 360 and which U.S. district court decided this case? ***Allen v. Men's World Outlet, Inc. – S.D.N.Y.***

9. What is the name of the case located at 54 F.R.D. 282 (W.D. Pa. 1971) and briefly state the topic the case discusses.

   ***United States v. Satan and His Staff*, which discusses an alleged violation of the plaintiff's civil rights. Satan allegedly caused the plaintiff misery and deprived him of his constitutional rights. The court found there was no jurisdiction.**

10. In which National Reporter System series do the decisions of the following states appear?

Kentucky	**Southwestern Reporter**
Ohio	**Northeastern Reporter**
Connecticut	**Atlantic Reporter**

11. Give the name of the case located at:

    a. 622 N.W.2d 1   ***State v. Davis***

    b. 272 S.E.2d 706   ***Benson v. York***

    c. 195 So. 248   ***Lang v. City of Mobile***

12. Give the parallel citations for the case located at 116 S. Ct. 356.

    516 U.S. 29, 133 L. Ed. 2d 271

13. Locate the case at 121 S. Ct. 447. How does page 39 of the parallel *United States Reports* begin? **It begins with the words "border itself."**

14. Locate the case at 144 L. Ed. 2d 196. How does page 219 of the parallel *United States Reports* begin? **It begins with the words "court action."**

15. Use the *National Reporter Blue Book* (2005 Cum. Supp.) and give the parallel citations for the following cases.

    a. 252 Ga. Ct. App. 45   **555 S.E.2d 506**

    b. 165 N.J. 205   **756 A.2d 1012**

    c. 167 Or. Ct. App. 1   **1 P.3d 1042**

16. Locate the case in 535 S.E.2d in which the defendant's name is *Traino*.

    a. Give the citation.   **535 S.E.2d 275 (Ga. Ct. App. 2000)**

    b. Who represented the appellant in this case? **Michael E. Garner**

    c. Who was the Chief Judge of the Georgia Court of Appeals during the period of time covered by this volume? **Edward H. Johnson**

Name _____

State Your Answer – Chapter Four
(xx points)

1. Use either the *Bluebook* or *ALWD* and identify the names of the sets of books that report case decisions from your state's courts.

    California: *California Reports*
    California Appellate Reports
    California Appellate Reports Supplement (bound with Cal. App.)
    Pacific Reporter
    California Reporter

    Florida: *Florida Reports* (only published until 1948)
    Southern Reporter
    Florida Supplement

    New York: *New York Reports*
    North Eastern Reporter
    New York Supplement
    New York Appellate Division Reports
    New York Miscellaneous Reports

    Texas: *Texas Reports* (only published until 1962)
    South Western Reporter
    Texas Cases ("West offprint" identified by *ALWD* but not by *Bluebook*)
    Texas Criminal Reports
    Texas Civil Appeals Reports
    (Note: Some older sets of books are also identified by the *Bluebook*.)

2. Use either the *Bluebook* or *ALWD* and prepare the following citation (assume it is being cited in an internal office memorandum at your firm):
    Anderson v. Diaz, a case decided by your state's highest court in 2003 and reported in volume 709, at page 404 of the relevant reporter.

    California: *Anderson v. Diaz*, 709 P.3d 404 (Cal. 2003)
    Florida: *Anderson v. Diaz*, 709 So. 2d 404 (Fla. 2003
    New York: *Anderson v. Diaz*, 709 N.E.2d 404 (N.Y. 2003)
    Texas: *Anderson v. Diaz*, 709 S.W.3d 404 (Tex. 2003)

3. Access the site for the Center for Individual Freedom (http://www.centerforindividualfreedom.org) and select "Legal" and review the statistics for the 2003 term of the United States Supreme Court. What was the reversal rate (expressed as a percentage) for your circuit during the 2003 term?

> **Reversal rates are found at:**
> **http://www.centerforindividualfreedom.org/legal/supreme_court_wary_of_9th/reversal_rates.pdf**
> | | |
> |---|---|
> | **Second Circuit (NY):** | **100%** |
> | **Fifth Circuit (TX):** | **100%** |
> | **Ninth Circuit (CA):** | **76%** |
> | **Eleventh Circuit (FL):** | **100%** |

4. Access the site MegaLaw at http://www.megalaw.com and select "State Law." Locate the site for your state's courts or judicial system and determine which court rules can be accessed through your state's site.

> | | |
> |---|---|
> | **California:** | **Ninth Circuit rules, federal district court local rules, federal bankruptcy court local rules, California state supreme court and appellate court rules, California state trial court rules** |
> | **Florida:** | **Fifth Circuit rules, rules of appellate procedure, civil procedure, criminal procedure, family law, judicial administration, probate, small claims, traffic court, workers compensation, and bar rules, and circuit court rules for various circuits** |
> | **New York:** | **Second Circuit rules, federal district court rules, federal bankruptcy court rules, unified court system local rules and their amendments, various individual judges rules, and rules of court of appeals** |
> | **Texas:** | **Fifth Circuit rules, federal district court rules, federal bankruptcy court rules, appellate procedure rules, rules of judicial conduct, court reporter rules, rules of civil evidence, civil procedure, criminal procedure, discovery, evidence, judicial administration, rules governing attorneys, rules governing parental notification, and rules history information** |

Name _____

Assignment for Chapter Five
(xx points)

1. Use the Table of Cases for the *Eleventh Decennial, Part 1*.

   a. Under which topic and key numbers is the following case digested: *Trecom Business Systems, Inc. v. Prasad*? **Contracts 160; Copyright 107, 109; and Federal Civil Procedure 2492**

   b. Give the citation to the case in which the defendant's name is *Derokey*. **729 So. 2d 654 (La. App. 1999)**

2. Use the Descriptive Word Index to the *Eleventh Decennia, Part 1*.

   a. Which topic and key number discuss lethal injection as a mode of execution in death penalty cases? **Sentencing and Punishment 1796**

   b. Look up this topic and key number in the *Eleventh Decennial, Part 1*. Which 1999 case from Arizona discusses this? *State v. Sharp*, **973 P.2d 1171, 193 Ariz. 414 (1999)**

3. Use the Descriptive Word Index to the *Tenth Decennial, Part 2*.

   a. Which topic and key number discuss games as nuisances? **Nuisances 3 (9)**

   b. Look up this topic and key number in the *Tenth Decennial, Part 2*. Which 1991 Nebraska case discusses this general topic? *Kaiser v. Western R/C Flyers, Inc.*, **477 N.W.2d 557, 239 Neb. 624 (1991)**

   c. Which 1997 Rhode Island case updates this? *Hennessey v. Pyne*, **694 A.2d 691 (R.I. 1997)**

4. Use West's set *Federal Practice Digest, 4th Series*.

   a. Which topic and key number discuss a right to a jury trial in employment discrimination cases? **Jury 14 (1.5)**

   b. Review this topic and key number. Which 2003 case from the Eighth Circuit ruled on this issue? *Harris v. Interstate Brands Corp.*, **348 F.3d 761 (8th Cir. 2003) [Note: This answer is found in pocket part.]**

c. Review this case. Was the plaintiff entitled to a jury trial in this matter? Why or why not? **No, plaintiff was not entitled to a jury because matter was decided by summary judgment, which was proper in this case, and which was held not to have violated the plaintiff's Seventh Amendment rights.**

5. Use West's set *United States Supreme Court Digest*. Give the citations to the case *Bayne v. Wiggins*. **11 S. Ct. 521, 139 U.S. 210, 35 L. Ed. 144.**

6. Use West's *Atlantic Digest 2d*.

   a. Which topic and key number discuss the use of expert witnesses in battered women's syndrome cases? **Criminal Law 474.4 (3)**

   b. Review the topic and key number. Give the name of the 1981 Maine case that discusses this issue and tell whether the expert witness testimony was permitted. **Yes, it was permitted.** *State v. Anaya*, **438 A.2d 892 (Me. 1981).**

7. Use A.L.R. *Quick Index* for A.L.R.3d, A.L.R.4th, and A.L.R.5th. Find and cite the annotations that relate to the following issues:

   a. Liability of a nursery school and day care center for injury to a child attending the facility (specifically, for injury caused by a crib). **58 A.L.R.4th 240.**

   b. Liability of dog owners for emotional injuries sustained by persons frightened by the owners' dogs. **30 A.L.R.4th 986.**

8. Review the above annotations, and answer the following questions:

   a. For 7(a) generally, which is the most recent case from the Georgia Court of Appeals in which negligence was established and the *res ipsa loquitur* doctrine was not at issue? ***Bull St. Church of Christ v. Jensen*, 233 Ga. App. 96, 504 S.E.2d 1 (1998) [Note: This case appears in a pocket part. An earlier case, *Jones v. Jones* is from 1969 and appears in the hardbound volume.]**

   b. For 7(b), cite a 1932 California Court of Appeals case that generally relates to this topic. ***Hicks v. Sullivan*, 122 Cal. App. 635, 10 P.2d 516 (1932)**

9. Use West's set *Words and Phrases*. What cases construe the meaning of the phrase "nurturing parent doctrine"? Give case names only. *Frankenfield v. Feeser, Depp v. Holland,* **and** *Woskob v. Woskob* **[*Woskob* is in pocket part.]**

Name_____

State Your Answer – Chapter Five
(xx points)

1. Access West's website at http://www.west.thomson.com. Select "Product Type" and then "Digests" and locate the digest for your state. Use the format "West's Iowa Digest" if you have difficulty. How often is your state's digest updated?

   California, Florida, and New York's digests are updated annually with cumulative supplements. Texas's digest is updated biannually with a cumulative supplement and annually with pocket parts.

2. Access the site MegaLaw at http://www.megalaw.com. Use "State Law" to access authorities and information for your state. Review "State Government Information" for your state.

   a. Identify your state's lieutenant governor.

California:	Lt. Gov. Cruz M. Bustamante, born in San Joaquin, CA.
Florida:	Lt. Gov. Toni Jennings, born in Orlando. FL.
New York:	Lt. Gov. Mary O. Donohue. No information given regarding her place of birth.
Texas:	Lt. Gov. David Dewhurst, a native of Texas.

   b. Identify whether your lieutenant is a native of your state. **See above.**

3. Access West's website at http://www.west.thomson.com.

   a. Select "User Guides" and then review a User Guide entitled "Using Secondary Sources." How does West describe A.L.R. on page 1 of this User Guide?

   "ALR Annotations: Encyclopedic essays (annotations) on the general topic discussed in key cases. These annotations are full of citations to cases, statutes, and secondary materials."

   b. Using the "Search Products" box, search for *Words and Phrases*. Review the product information about this set, specifically its "Summary of Contents." What words and phrases does Volume 37 (also called Book 86) cover?
   Volume 37 covers "Repay – Res ipsa."

Name

Assignment for Chapter Six
(xx points)

1. Use Am. Jur. 2d.

    a. Which volume, title, and section deal with gambling on sports events?

    38 Am. Jur. 2d *Gambling* § 79

    b. Review this section. What exceptions exist to the federal statute prohibiting gambling on sporting events? **Exceptions exist for systems in operation before certain dates, jai alai, and pari-mutuel betting on animal races.**

2. Use Am. Jur. 2d.

    a. Which volume, title, and section deal with chickens as nuisances?

    4 Am. Jur. 2d *Animals* § 72

    b. Review this section. Which Massachusetts case held that noises and odors from a chickenhouse and yard maintained in a clean manner are not a nuisance? *Wade v. Miller*, **188 Mass. 6, 73 N.E. 849**

3. Use C.J.S.

    a. Use the Table of Cases. Under which topic and section is the case *Albertson v. Leca* discussed? ***Taxation* § 1104**

    b. Which topic and section discuss cruelty as grounds for divorce? ***Divorce* § 22**

    c. Review the above section. What happens if both parties are guilty of habitual cruel and inhuman treatment?

    It is the duty of the court to determine which party's conduct is the proximate cause of the divorce.

    d. Give a short summary of the definition of "release." **The relinquishment, concession, or giving up of a right, claim, or privilege.**

4. Use *Am. Jur. Proof of Facts (3d)*.

   a. Give the citation to an article relating to the availability of punitive damages in an automobile accident with a school bus. **17 P.O.F.3d 311, § 17**

   b. Review the above section. What South Carolina case(s) discuss(es) this? Give the case name(s) only. ***Fisher v. J.H. Sheridan Co., Samuel v. Mouzon***

   c. Who authored this article? **Russell L. Wald, L.L.B.**

5. Use *Index to Legal Periodicals & Books* to answer the following questions:

   a. Cite an article written by Ann Laquer Estin in spring 2002 relating to marriage. **100 No. 6 Mich. L. Rev. 1690-707 – May 2002**

   b. Cite an article written in late 2003 relating to end-stage anorexia and competence to refuse treatment. **International Journal of Law & Psychiatry, v. 26, no. 6, pp. 677-95, N/D '03**

   c. Cite an article published in the winter of 2002 about a case in which the defendant's name is *Gilmore*. **59, no. 1 Wash. & Lee Law Rev. 299-360**

6. Use the Subject Index for *Current Law Index* for 2003 and give the citation to an article relating to school busing. ***Redlining Learners: Delaware's Neighborhood Schools*, 20 Delaware Lawyer 14 (19) Fall 2002**

7. Give the title and the authors of the April 2003 law review article located at 81 Tex. L. Rev. 1177. ***The Rise of the Personal Animosity Presumption in Title VII and the Return to "No Cause" Employment* by Chad Derum and Karen Engle**

8. Use *J. Thomas McCarthy on Trademarks and Unfair Competition* (4th ed. 1996)

   a. What section discusses "puffing" as false advertising? **§27:38**

   b. Review the section. Is a claim that a product is "better" than another product false advertising? Why or why not? **Such a claim is not false advertising because it is too vague.**

9. Use *Williston on Contracts* (Richard A. Lord ed., 4th ed. 1990).

   a. What section discusses rejection of goods for defective quality? **§ 40:10**

   b. Review this section. May a buyer reject goods for deficient quality where the buyer has failed to provide specifications needed by the seller to determine and meet the alleged quality standards? Provide an answer and cite the best case in support of your answer. **No.** *Ez-Tixz Inc. v. Hit-Tix*, **969 F. Supp. 220 (S.D.N.Y. 1997)**

10. Use *Restatement (Third) of Trusts*.

    a. What section discusses the removal of a trustee, generally? **§ 37**

    b. Review this section. How may a trustee be removed? **A trustee may be removed in accord with the terms of the trust or for cause by a proper court.**

    c. Review the Reporter's Notes for this section (specifically, comment e). May a trustee be removed for habitual drunkenness in Ohio? Provide an answer and cite the relevant statute in support of your answer. **Yes. Ohio Rev. Code § 2109.24**

Name _____

State Your Answer – Chapter Six
(xx points)

1. Access the Web site for Georgetown University Law Center at www.ll.georgetown.edu. Select "Learn" and then "Tutorials." Review the information given on encyclopedias. Which of the two national or general encyclopedias does this site recommend as a starting place? Why?

    This site states that Am. Jur. 2d is a better starting place because the information in the bound volumes is usually more current than the text in C.J.S.

2. Access the University Law Review Project at www.lawreview.org. Select "General Law Reviews." What law reviews from your state are now available through this site?

    Answers will vary. After accessing the site, users will be directed to the following site: http://stu.findlaw.com/journals/general.html.

3. Access the Washington & Lee Law School study on the most cited legal periodicals at www.wlu.edu.library/research/lawrevs/mostcited.asp. Sort the table by rank. As of 2003, which were the top four most-cited periodicals? How many times was each cited?

    The most frequently cited periodicals, in order are Harvard (with 6,682 references), Yale (with 5,582 references), Columbia (with 4,742 references), and Stanford (with 4,262 references).

4. Access the site of the American Law Institute at www.ali.org and review ALI's annual report for 2004. Review the table that indicates how many times published cases cite to the Restatements.
    a. How many times has your state cited the Restatement of Torts as of March 1, 2003?

California	**4,060**
Florida	**1,226**
New York	**2,314**
Texas	**2,244**

    b. What is the most frequently cited Restatement in your state?

    In each of the above states, the Restatement of Torts is cited more frequently than any other Restatement.

216

                                                                    Name
                        Assignment for Chapter Seven
                                 (xx points)

1. Use *Black's Law Dictionary* (8th ed. 2004).

    a. What is the definition of "motion to suppress"?
        A request that the court prohibit the introduction of illegally obtained evidence at a criminal trial.

    b. What topic and key number are you directed to relating to this definition?
        Criminal Law 394.6

    c. What does the legal maxim *fructus pendentes pars fundi videntur* mean?
        "Hanging fruits are considered part of the parcel of land."

2. Use the most current edition of *Martindale-Hubbell Law Directory*.

    a. An attorney named Hugh L. Wilcox, Jr. is with the Florence, South Carolina firm of Wilcox, Buyck & Williams. Where and when did Mr. Wilcox attend law school? **University of South Carolina, J.D. 1971**

    b. Review the Corporate Law Departments volume. What corporation employs Catrina McLean? **Dynegy Inc. of Houston**

    c. An attorney named Philippe Beurier is with the Paris, France law firm Bredin Prat. Where did he receive his law degree? **University of Paris Law School**

    d. What is the filing fee in North Carolina for filing articles of incorporation for a corporation? **$125**

    e. Review the ABA Model Rules of Professional Conduct. What Rule relates to confidentiality of information? **Rule 1.6**

    f. In China, how long does software copyright protection last? **Protection lasts 25 years (but owner may apply for an extension of another 25 years, but maximum protection shall not be longer than 50 years).**

    g. Review the Uniform Arbitration Act. What does § 13 cover?
        Modification or correction of arbitration award or action by majority (2000 Act)

3. Use *Am. Jur. Legal Forms (2d)*.

   a. What forms relate to the payment of moving expenses in employment contracts? **Forms 99:103 and 99:104**

   b. Review the first form. What Am. Jur. 2d reference are you given? **27 Am. Jur. 2d *Employment Relationship* § 52 et seq.**

4. Use *Am. Jur. Pleading and Practice Forms Annotated*.

   a. What form provides a complaint against a bar or tavern owner for an attack by an intoxicated mob? **Mob 7**

   b. Review the complaint. What does Paragraph 1 allege? **Plaintiff's residency**

   c. What form provides a complaint against a cosmetic surgeon for facial disfigurement? **Phys 507**

   d. Review the complaint. What does Paragraph 7 allege? **Actress's lips and mouth are ugly, unsightly, and disproportionate to her face, due to defendant's negligence in making her lips droop.**

5. Use *Uniform Laws Annotated*.

   a. Has Utah adopted the Uniform Probate Code (1969)? **Yes**

   b. If so, give the citation to Utah's statute. **U.C.A. 1953, 75-1-101 to 75-8-101**

   c. Review the Uniform Probate Code. What is the general topic of section 2-907? **Honorary Trusts; Trusts for Pets**

   d. Review section 2-907. Generally, is a trust for the care of a designated animal valid? **Yes**

Name _____

State Your Answer – Chapter Seven
(xx points)

1. Access the Web site for the National Association of Attorneys General at http://www.naag.org and identify the attorney general for your state.

   California: **Bill Lockyer**
   Florida: **Charlie Crist**
   New York: **Eliot Spitzer**
   Texas: **Greg Abbott**

2. Access the online legal dictionary at http://dictionary.law.com and provide the definition for "nunc pro tunc."

   The phrase is Latin for "now for then" and refers to changing back to an earlier date of an order, judgment, or filing of a document.

3. Access the Web site for the National Conference of Commissioners on Uniform State Laws at http://www.nccusl.org/update/AboutNCCUSL_desktopdefault.aspx and identify the commissioners from your state.

   California

   Beverly, Robert G.
   Bosco, Cynthia
   Boyer-Vine, Diane
   Burke, William M.
   Cornell, Robert H.
   Deblase, Patrick
   Gregory, Bion M.
   Harman, Tom
   Harris, Elihu M.
   Mandel, Elaine
   Park, Ann I.
   Rae, Jr., Matthew S.
   Recht, Phil
   Sher, Byron D.
   Sterling, Nathaniel
   Willoughby, W. Jackson

   Florida
   Cutler, Edward I.
   Ehrhardt, Charles W.
   Jessen, Linda S.

Kittleson, Henry M.
Morse, III, Joshua M.
Stagg, C. Lawrence

New York

Elacqua, Jamie-Lynn
Greene, Norman L.
Long, Richard B.
Stern, Sandra S.
Vigdor, Justin L.

Texas

Auld, Marianne
Benton, Levi
Godbey, David
Guillot, Patrick C.
Munson, Peter K.
Phelan, Marilyn E.
Plettman, Stanley
Reese, Leonard
Satterwhite, Rodney W.
Tindall, Harry L.
Washington, Karen Roberts
Yeakel, Lee

4. Access MegaLaw at http://www.megalaw.com and select "Legal Forms" and then "Secretary of State Forms." What is the filing fee in your state for filing articles of incorporation (to incorporate a business) for a stock or "for profit" corporation?

California:	$100
Florida:	$35 (plus $35 for the designation of the registered agent)
New York:	$125
Texas:	$300

5. Access the article "What is the Law? Finding Jury Instructions" at http://www.llrx.com/columns/reference19.htm and determine whether your state's jury instructions are available online.

California:	Yes
Florida:	Yes (Statewide Jury Instructions, Ninth Judicial Circuit Court)
New York:	Yes (Criminal jury instructions are available)
Texas:	No

Name _____

Answer Keys – Chapter Eight
(xx points)

[*Bluebook* format – note that where italics appear, underscoring would be acceptable.]

1. Vincent Amato, Jr. v. Randall F. Cochran, a 1990 Rhode Island Supreme Court case found in volume 601 at page 224 of the relevant reporter.

    Amato v. Cochran, 601 A.2d 224 (R.I. 1990)

2. Anderson General Construction Company v. Candy Benner, a Michigan Supreme Court case decided in 2001, located in volume 664 at page 14.

    Anderson General Construction Co. v. Benner, 664 N.W.2d 14 (Mich. 2001)

3. Michael J. Finnegan versus Teresa Finnegan, a 1994 case from the Georgia Court of Appeals, located in volume 607 of the relevant reporter, page 903, with quoted material on pages 914 to 916.

    Finnegan v. Finnegan, 607 S.E.2d 903, 914-16 (Ga. Ct. App. 1994)

4. Douglas Consolidated Corporation vs. Flynn Brothers, 502 United States Reports 16, 329 Lawyers' Edition (Second Series) page 789, 319 Supreme Court Reporter page 906.

    Douglas Consolidated Corp. v. Flynn Bros., 502 U.S. 16 (year)

5. Federal Communications Commission v. Anne Griffin, Richard Garcia, and Diana Francois, 145 Federal Reporter (Third Series) 886.

    FCC v. Griffin, 145 F.3d 886 (xxx Cir. year)
    [Note that the *Bluebook* would permit "FCC" to be spelled out.]

6. USA v. Mark Gage, Trustee, 114 Federal Supplement (Second Series) 423, decided in the District Court for the District of Columbia.

    United States v. Gage, 114 F. Supp. 2d 423 (D.D.C. year)

7. Gunther Association v. Andrea Chu, a 2003 Supreme Court case.

   ***Gunther Ass'n v. Chu,* xxx U.S. xxx (2003)**

8. Title 42, United States Code, Sections 2244 through 2248.

   42 U.S.C. §§ 2244-2248 (2000)

9. Title 15, U.S.C.A. Section 109.

   15 U.S.C.A. § 109 (West year)

10. Title 35 U.S.C.S. Section 1561(a).

    35 U.S.C.S. § 1561(a) (LexisNexis year)

11. Section 15-455 of the Idaho Code.

    Idaho Code Ann. § 15-455 (year)

12. Section **22-013 of Maryland's Health Occupations Code.**

    Md. Code Ann., Health Occ. § 22-013 (LexisNexis [or West] year)

13. Fourth Amendment to the United States Constitution.

    U.S. Const. amend. IV

14. Section 3-211 of Restatement (Second Series) of Contracts.

    Restatement (Second) of Contracts § 3-211 (year)

15. An article by Kelly Gray and Richard P. King entitled "Calculating Loss of Consortium," published in volume 42 of the South Carolina Law Review, at page 1054, with a quotation from pages 1062 through 1068.

    Kelly Gray & Richard P. King, *Calculating Loss of Consortium*, 42 S.C. L. Rev. 1054, 1062-68 (year)

16. Volume 6, Section 14:10 of the second edition of the treatise authored by Kevin Bidwell entitled "A Practitioner's Guide to Family Law."

    6 Kevin Bidwell, *A Practitioner's Guide to Family Law* § 14:10 (2d ed. year)

17. Assume the following case is cited in a brief to a Massachusetts state court that requires parallel citations: Reynolds v. Patty Shaw, 309 Massachusetts Appeals Court 109. Give the correct citation.

> ***Reynolds v. Shaw*, 309 Mass. App. Ct. 109, xxx N.E.2d xxx (App. Ct. year)**
>
> **[Note to Instructors: See the examples on pages 9 and 90 of *the Bluebook* for analogous state court of appeals cases and the reference on page 214 showing that the abbreviation for the set *Massachusetts Appeals Court Reports* is "Mass. App. Ct."]**

18. Assume the following citation appears as a "stand alone" citation: the 2004 United States Court of Appeals case from the Third Circuit entitled Reynolds Restaurant Division Inc. v. Northern Maintenance Management Company. Give the correct citation.

> ***Reynolds Rest. Div. Inc. v. N. Maint. Mgmt. Co.*, xxx F.3d xxx (3d Cir. 2004)**

19. The definition of "negligence" appearing on page 450 of the current edition of Black's Law Dictionary.

> ***Black's Law Dictionary* 450 (8th ed. 2004)**

[*ALWD* format – Note that where italics appear, underscoring would be acceptable.]
(xx points)

1. Vincent Amato, Jr. v. Randall F. Cochran, a 1990 Rhode Island Supreme Court case found in volume 601 at page 224 of the relevant reporter.

   Amato v. Cochran, 601 A.2d 224 (R.I. 1990)

2. Anderson General Construction Company v. Candy Benner, a Michigan Supreme Court case decided in 2001, located in volume 664 at page 14.

   Anderson General Construction Co. v. Benner, 664 N.W.2d 14 (Mich. 2001)

3. Michael J. Finnegan versus Teresa Finnegan, a 1994 case from the Georgia Court of Appeals, located in volume 607 of the relevant reporter, page 903, with quoted material on pages 914 to 916.

   Finnegan v. Finnegan, 607 S.E.2d 903, 914-16 (Ga. App. 1994)
   [Note that *ALWD* also permits the span of pages as "914-916."]

4. Douglas Consolidated Corporation vs. Flynn Brothers, 502 United States Reports 16, 329 Lawyers' Edition (Second Series) page 789, 319 Supreme Court Reporter page 906.

   Douglas Consolidated Corp. v. Flynn Bros., 502 U.S. 16 (year)
   [Note that *ALWD* also permits all parallel citations, as follows:
   502 U.S. 16, 310 S. Ct. 906, 329 L. Ed. 2d 789 (year).]

5. Federal Communications Commission v. Anne Griffin, Richard Garcia, and Diana Francois, 145 Federal Reporter (Third Series) 886.

   FCC v. Griffin, 145 F.3d 886 (xxx Cir. year)

6. USA v. Mark Gage, Trustee, 114 Federal Supplement (Second Series) 423, decided in the District Court for the District of Columbia.

   U.S. v. Gage, 114 F. Supp. 2d 423 (D.D.C. year)

7. Gunther Association v. Andrea Chu, a 2003 Supreme Court case.

> *Gunter Assn v. Chu*, xxx U.S. xxx (2003)
> [Note that *ALWD* permits parallel cites.]

8. Title 42, United States Code, Sections 2244 through 2248.

> **42 U.S.C. §§ 2244-2248 (2000)**

9. Title 15, U.S.C.A. Section 109.

> **15 U.S.C.A. § 109 (West year)**

10. Title 35 U.S.C.S. Section 1561(a).

> **35 U.S.C.S. § 1561(a) (LEXIS year)**

11. Section 15-455 of the Idaho Code.

> **Idaho Code § 15-455 (year)**

12. Section 22-013 of Maryland's Health Occupations Code.

> **Md. Health Occs. Code Ann. § 22-013 (year)**

13. Fourth Amendment to the United States Constitution.
    U.S. Const. amend. IV

14. Section 3-211 of Restatement (Second Series) of Contracts.

> *Restatement (Second) of Contracts* § 3-211 (year)

15. An article by Kelly Gray and Richard P. King entitled "Calculating Loss of Consortium," published in volume 42 of the South Carolina Law Review, at page 1054, with a quotation from pages 1062 through 1068.

> **Kelly Gray & Richard P. King,** *Calculating Loss of Consortium*, **42 S.C. L. Rev. 1054, 1062-68 (year)**
> [Note that *ALWD* would permit "1062-1068."]

16. Volume 6, Section 14:10 of the second edition of the treatise authored by Kevin Bidwell entitled "A Practitioner's Guide to Family Law."

> **Kevin Bidwell,** *A Practitioner's Guide to Family Law* **vol. 6, § 14:10 (2d ed., Publisher year)**

17. Assume the following case is cited in a brief to a Massachusetts state court that requires parallel citations: Reynolds v. Patty Shaw, 309 Massachusetts Appeals Court 109. Give the correct citation.

Reynolds v. Shaw, 309 Mass. App. 109, xxx N.E.2d xxx (year)

18. Assume the following citation appears as a "stand alone" citation: the 2004 United States Court of Appeals case from the Third Circuit entitled Reynolds Restaurant Division Inc. v. Northern Maintenance Management Company. Give the correct citation.

Reynolds Rest. Div. Inc. v. N. Maint. Mgt. Co., xxx F.3d xxx (3d Cir. 2004)

19. The definition of "negligence" appearing on page 450 of the current edition of Black's Law Dictionary.

Black's Law Dictionary 450 (Bryan A. Garner ed., 8th ed., West 2004)

Memorandum Assignment for Chapter Eight - *Bluebook* format
(xx points)

The general rule is that shareholders of a corporation receive dividends when and if declared by the board of directors acting in its discretion. *Allen Ass'n v. Taylor Corp.*, 523 U.S. 16, xx (1988). Thus, the determination to distribute dividends is a discretionary decision subject to the business judgment of the directors. *Id.* at 23. The directors may properly decide that dividends should not be paid so that the corporation can build up a "war chest" to acquire another corporation, for purposes of growth and expansion, or for the purpose of investing its profits. *Sanderson v. Bailey Bros. Corp.*, 29 F.3d 250, 251-54 (2d Cir.), *aff'd*, 530 U.S. 62 (2001). The mere fact that the corporation has sufficient funds from which to pay a dividend does not entitle the shareholders to a dividend. *Id.*

The articles of incorporation may provide for a fixed dividend to one class or series of shares. **Cal. Corp. Code § 8023 (West [or Deering] year).** In such a case, the directors will be required to declare the agreed-upon dividend when legally available funds exist. **Catherine Leonard, *Corporate Investment* §§ 36-41 (3d ed. 1999).** If the dividends are cumulative, any arrearages must be paid for prior years in which the corporation did not pay dividends, before any dividends can be paid to other (usually common) shareholders. **Cal. Corp. Code § 8023.**

Courts are reluctant to interfere with the management of corporations, and, therefore, unless the shareholders can clearly prove bad faith or an abuse of discretion by the directors, the directors cannot be compelled to pay dividends. **Leonard, *supra*, § xx.** This is yet another example of the business judgment rule, which protects directors who make business decisions in good faith. *Id.* As a practical matter, however, directors who fail to declare dividends when profits permit may well find themselves out of a job.

Memorandum for Chapter Eight - *ALWD* format
(xx points)

The general rule is that shareholders of a corporation receive dividends when and if declared by the board of directors acting in its discretion. *Allen Assn v. Taylor Corp.*, 523 U.S. 16, xx (1988) [Note that *ALWD* permits parallel citations.]. Thus, the determination to distribute dividends is a discretionary decision subject to the business judgment of the directors. *Id.* at 23. The directors may properly decide that dividends should not be paid so that the corporation can build up a "war chest" to acquire another corporation, for purposes of growth and expansion, or for the purpose of investing its profits. *Sanderson v. Bailey Bros. Corp.*, 29 F.3d 250, 251-54 [or "251-254"] (2d Cir. 2001), *aff'd*, 530 U.S. 62 (2001). The mere fact that the corporation has sufficient funds from which to pay a dividend does not entitle the shareholders to a dividend. *Id.*

The articles of incorporation may provide for a fixed dividend to one class or series of shares. Cal. Corps. Code Ann. § 8023 (West [or LEXIS] year). In such a case, the directors will be required to declare the agreed-upon dividend when legally available funds exist. Catherine Leonard, *Corporate Investment* §§ 36-41 (3d ed., Publisher 1999). If the dividends are cumulative, any arrearages must be paid for prior years in which the corporation did not pay dividends, before any dividends can be paid to other (usually common) shareholders. Cal. Corps. Code § 8023.

Courts are reluctant to interfere with the management of corporations, and, therefore, unless the shareholders can clearly prove bad faith or an abuse of discretion by the directors, the directors cannot be compelled to pay dividends. Leonard, *supra* § xx, at xx. This is yet another example of the business judgment rule, which protects directors who make business decisions in good faith. *Id.* As a practical matter, however, directors who fail to declare dividends when profits permit may well find themselves out of a job.

Name _____

State Your Answer – Chapter Eight
(xx points)

1. Review the Universal Citation Guide Version 2.1 at www.aallnet.org/committee/citationucg/index.html. Review Paragraph 29. In what way do the AALL Proposal and the ABA model for universal citation forms differ?

    The AALL and the ABA use different abbreviations for courts. The court abbreviation data elements differ.

2. Access the ABA site relating to universal citation form at www.abanet.org/tech/ltrc/research/citation/home.html and review ABA Citation History.

    a. When was the first draft report on citation reform submitted?

    March 18, 1986

    b. What did this report recommend?

    The report recommended that all jurisdictions adopt a system for citation to case reports that would be equally effective for printed case reports and for case reports published on computer discs or network services.

3. Access the ABA site relating to universal citation form and review the information related to Wisconsin. What action has Wisconsin taken with regard to universal citation form?

    In the Supreme Court of Wisconsin and the Court of Appeals, the official publication of each opinion published after January 1, 2000, shall set forth the public domain citation and include the paragraph numbering of the opinion.

4. Access the site of the Association of Legal Writing Directors at www.alwd.org. Select "ALWD Citation Manual" and review Chart 12.7

    a. List the divisions of your state's appellate courts.

    b. Are decisions of one court binding on other intermediate courts?

    <u>California</u>: **Court of Appeals, First through Sixth Districts. Appellate courts do not bind each other. When appellate**

courts disagree, a lower court may choose the most persuasive decision.

Florida: District Court of Appeals, First through Fifth. District courts of appeal do not bind each other; however, the trial court sitting within a district of appeal that has not ruled on the issue at hand is bound by the decisions of other district courts of appeal.

New York: Supreme Court Appellate Division, First through Fourth Departments. Appellate courts do not bind each other. A lower court must follow decisions of the appellate division in its department. If an appellate division hasn't ruled on an issue, it is bound by a decision of a department that has ruled on the issue. If other departments are in conflict, the lower court may render an appropriate decision.

Texas: Court of Appeals, First through Fourteenth Districts. No, appellate courts do not bind each other. Note that Texas also has two courts of last resort: the Texas Supreme Court and the Court of Criminal Appeals.

Name _____

Assignment for Chapter Nine
(xx points)

1. Shepardize 620 A.2d 485.

   a. Give the parallel citation. **533 Pa. 124**

   b. Review the abbreviations in the front of this volume. What does "NJL" stand for? **New Jersey Law Reports**

2. Locate Shepard's first reference to 179 N.W. 81.

   a. Give the parallel citation. **190 Ia 848**

   b. What is the first case that follows headnote 3 of 179 N.W. 81?
   f 179 N.W.2d ₃ 156

   c. What is the most recent A.L.R. annotation in this volume that mentions this case? **2 A.L.R.3d 686n**

   d. Review the abbreviations in the front of the volume. What does "CoLR" stand for? **Construction Litigation Reports (Shepard's)**

3. Shepardize 692 N.E.2d 369.

   a. Give the parallel citations. **295 Ill. App. Ct. 3d 90, 229 Ill. Dec. 596**

   b. Has this case ever been questioned? If so, give the citation.
   Yes. q 705N.E.2d 955

4. Locate the first time Shepard's discusses 331 S.E.2d 846.

   a. Give the parallel citation. **175 W. Va. 115**

   b. What negative treatment is given for this case in this volume?
   o 403 S.E.2d 400

5. Locate the first time Shepard's discusses 736 P.2d 161.

   a. Give the name of the case. *Moore v. Oklahoma*

   b. Give the citations to the denial of *certiorari* for 736 P.2d 161.
   484 U.S. 873, 108 S. Ct. 212

c. What case was connected with 736 P.2d 161? **809 P.2d 63**

6. Use *Shepard's Southwestern Citations, Cases and Case Names* (hard cover volume, volume 2, part 6, for 2001). Locate the entries for 842 S.W.2d 704.

    a. Give the name of the case. ***Edwards v. Holleman***

    b. What negative history is given for the case? **reversed 862 S.W.2d 580**

    c. Review the entries for 842 S.W.2d 580 in this volume. Was this case cited in a concurring opinion? If so, give the citation. **Yes ~ 876 S.W.2d ₁ 441**

7. Use *Shepard's Federal Citations* (hardcover supplement, volume 2 for 2003-2004. Locate the entries for 127 F.3d 632.

    a. Give the name of this case. ***Aliwoli v. Gilmore***

    b. What Sixth Circuit case followed headnote 3 of this 1997 case?
    f 324 F.3d ₃ 845

8. Use *Shepard's Federal Citations* for the first time Shepard's mentions 831 F. Supp. 1111.

    a. Was this case affirmed? If so, give the citation to the affirming case. **Yes, 46 F.3d 1116**

    b. Retrieve the volume for the case that affirmed 831 F. Supp. 1111. Was this affirming case published? **No – listed in table of unpublished decisions**

9. Use *Shepard's United States Citations* for the first time 529 U.S. 765 is mentioned and Shepardize 529 U.S. 765 in this volume. What A.L.R. Fed. annotation discusses this case? **187 A.L.R. Fed. 187n**

10. Use *Shepard's United States Citations* for the first time 468 U.S. 491 is mentioned and Shepardize 468 U.S. 91 in this volume. What was the first case to explain this case? **e 984 F.2d 1513**

11. Use *Shepard's Federal Statute Citations* for 1996-2001, volume 3, hardcover supplement, and Shepardize 36 U.S.C. § 5703. Give the negative history for this statute. **Repealed 112 St. 1499**

12. Use *Shepard's Federal Statute Citations* for 1996-2001, volume 1, hardcover supplement, and Shepardize 15 U.S.C. § 1052(f).

    a. Which Tenth Circuit case mentions this statute? **18 F. Supp. 2d 1206 Δ 1998**

    b. What does the delta symbol (Δ) in the citation mean? **The symbol means that the court did not specify which edition of U.S.C. it cited (but Shepard's tells that the citing case was decided in 1998)**

13. Use *Shepard's Federal Statute Citations* for 2001-2003, volume 1, hardcover supplement, for the U.S. Constitution. What is the first Fourth Circuit case to discuss clause one of Article Six? **255 F. Supp. 2d 549**

14. Use *Shepard's Federal Statute Citations* for 1996, for Tariff Schedules, Statutes at Large, and so forth.

    a. Shepardize Volume 23 of U.S. Treaties and Other International Agreements 3693. Give the history. **A TIAS 7560**

    b. Shepardize Rule 33 of the Rules of the Supreme Court of the United States. What Seventh Circuit case discusses this rule? **606 F.2d 168**

15. Use *Shepard's Acts and Cases by Popular Name (Federal and State)*, 1999, Pt. 3.

    a. Give the citation to the Happy Thought Case. **251 F. 301**

    b. Give the citation to the Sickle Cell Disease Detection Act. **Ky. Rev. Stat. 1971, 402.310 et seq.**

Name _____

State Your Answer – Chapter Nine
(xx points)

1. Access http://lexisnexis.com/shepards and select "Shepard's Citations in Print," and then "Features" and "Specialized Citators Table." What does *Shepard's* Federal Circuit Table do?

    This is a one-volume source to determine which federal or district court decided any federal court decision.

2. Access http://lexisnexis.com/shepards and select "Features." What two report formats can you select when you Shepardize online?

    You can select either FULL or KWIK formats. FULL retrieves all citing references while KWIK directs you to references that only relate to whether your case is still good law.

3. Access http://lexisnexis.com/shepards and select "*Shepard's* on LexisNexis at www.lexis.com," and then "Features," and then "Product Literature." Review William L. Taylor's article about *Shepard's* and KeyCite.

    a. What is the title of this article?

    The title is *Comparing KeyCite and Shepard's for Completeness, Currency, and Accuracy.*

    b. Review paragraph 29 of the article. What is Mr. Taylor's conclusion?

    Mr. Taylor concluded that to improve accuracy, researchers should check citations in both KeyCite and Shepard's online, remembering that between 10 and 37 percent of possible negative analyses were missed if a citation was checked in only one of the services.

4. Access www.westlaw.com and locate information on WestCheck.com. What three tasks does WestCheck.com perform automatically?

    WestCheck.com automatically extracts citations and applies KeyCite to citations from your document, retrieves KeyCite and Table of Authorities results, and retrieves will full text documents using Find.

Name _____

Assignment for Chapter Ten
(xx points)

LEGISLATIVE HISTORY

1. Use the CIS Annual Index for 2000.

    a. What public law relates to Internet false identification and prevention? **PL206-578**

    b. Locate the CIS "Legislative History" volume for this public law.

    (i) When was it approved? **Dec. 28, 2000**

    (ii) What was its designation in the Senate? **S 2924**

    (iii) What days did debate occur in the House and in the Senate? **In the Senate, debate occurred on October 31, 2000; in the House, debate occurred on December 15, 2000.**

2. Use the CIS Index for 2003.

    a. For what piece of legislation did Maria C. Lehman testify? **Federal Highway and Surface Transportation Programs Extension and Revision**

    b. Review the CIS Abstracts for 2003. What day did Ms. Lehman testify? **Feb. 28, 2002**

    c. Who is Ms. Lehman? **Commissioner, Public Works, Erie County, NY**

3. Use *United States Code Congressional and Administrative News*.

    a. To what topic does Public Law 108-110 relate? **Do Not Call Registry – Implementation by FTC**

    b. Use Table 9 for the 108th Congress, 1st Session. Locate information relating to the Authorization of Substitute Checks (Check Clearing for the 21st Century) Act.

    (i) Give the House Bill Number. **HR 1474**

    (ii) Give the date the bill was reported from the House. **June 2**

(iii) Give the date the bill was passed by the House. **June 5**

(iii) Give the date the bill was passed by the Senate. **June 27**

(iv) Give the date the bill was approved. **Oct. 28**

(v) Give the Public Law Number for this legislation. **PL 108-100**

4. Review the legislative history in *United States Code Congressional and Administrative News* for the above-identified Public Law.

   a. According to House Conference Report 108-291, page 19, what is the general purpose of this bill? **To facilitate check truncation by authorizing substitute checks and to foster innovation in the check collection system without mandating receipt of checks in electronic form and to improve the overall efficiency of the nation's payment system**

   b. What volume of the *Congressional Record* includes debates relating to this legislation? **Volume 149**

5. Review the *Congressional Record* for January 25, 2005.

   a. Who led the pledge of allegiance in the House? **Mr. Cuellar**

   b. Which chaplain offered the prayer in the Senate? **Dr. Barry C. Black**

   c. What anniversary was remembered in the Senate that day? **It was the 60th anniversary of the liberation of Auschwitz.**

ADMINISTRATIVE LAW AND PRESIDENTIAL DOCUMENTS

6. Use the most recent C.F.R. Index and Finding Aids volume.

   a. What C.F.R. title and part deal with school breakfast programs? **7 C.F.R. 220**

   b. What C.F.R. title and part deal with meat inspection, specifically, disposal of diseased carcasses? **9 C.F.R. 311**

      (i) Review this provision and its subparts. What happens if a carcass is affected by brucellosis? **Carcasses affected with localized lesions of brucellosis may be passed for human food after affecting parts are removed and condemned.**

(ii) Must anemic carcasses be condemned? **Yes, they must be condemned if they're too anemic to produce wholesome meat.**

7. Use the CCH *Blue Sky Reporter*.

    a. Use the Index. What section deals with the filing of proxy statements in annual reports? **Section 706**

    b. Review this section. When must copies of annual reports be furnished to the SEC?

    Copies must be furnished not later than the date on which the report is first sent or delivered to security holders or the date on which preliminary copies (or definitive copies if preliminary copies are not required to be filed) of solicitation material are filed with the SEC, whichever is later.

    c. Use the Table of Cases. What section discusses *Lasker v. Burks*? **§ 894**

    d. Review the section discussing *Lasker v. Burks*. What proposition does the case stand for?

    The Investment Advisers Act and Investment Company Act have been said to achieve the ends of high standards of ethics by interposing statutorily disinterested directors as a check on the actions of majority directors of investment companies controlled by investment advisers.

8. Use *Weekly Compilation of Presidential Documents*.

    a. Whose death was acknowledged on July 5, 2002? **Ted Williams**

    b. Review the "Exchange with Reporters" that occurred in Kennebunkport, Maine on July 6, 2002. Whose birthday was it that day? **It was the birthday of the President (George W. Bush)**

INTERNATIONAL LAW

9. Use the Cumulative Index, Volume 29/30 for volumes 1601-1700 for the United Nations Treaty Series. Find the treaty that deals with friendship and delimitation of the maritime boundary between the United States and the Cook Islands. When and where was the agreement signed? **June 11, 1980 - Rarotonga**

10. Use the Index for volumes 1301-1350 of the United Nations Treaty Series and find the agreement between Brazil and Argentina relating to animal health in the frontier area.

    a. Give the citations to the agreement. **I:22326; v:1331:3**

    b. When did the agreement enter into force? **7/1/83 [Note: answer is in footnote.]**

    c. When and where was the agreement signed? **It was signed on May 17, 1980 in Buenos Aires.**

    d. Who signed the agreement for each party? **Ramiro Saraiva Guerreiro signed for Brazil and Carlos W. Pastor signed for the Argentine Republic.**

    e. How long will the treaty remain in force? **It will remain in force for three years from the date of exchange of instruments of ratification and may be extended automatically for further three-year periods.**

11. Use Hackworth's *Digest of International Law*.

    a. What volume and page discuss hauling down or capture of a flag?

    VII:219

    b. Review this section.

    (i) Must a ship be fired upon or boarded to be captured? **No**

    (ii) When is a vessel taken as a prize? **when resistance has completely ceased**

12. Use Whiteman's *Digest of International Law*.

   a. What volume and page provide the definition of "shipwreck"? **11:389**

   b. Give the definition for "shipwreck." **"Shipwreck" means shipwreck from any cause and includes forced landings at sea by or from aircraft.**

13. Use U.S. Treaties and Other International Agreements. What is the general subject matter of 35 U.S.T. 1917 (T.I.A.S. 10769)? **Agricultural commodities in the Dominican Republic**

14. Use *Resolutions and Decisions Adopted by the General Assembly* for the first part of the 52nd Session of the United Nations in 1997.

   a. What is the general subject matter of the Resolution? **Women in Development**

   b. Was the Resolution adopted with or without a vote? **It was adopted without a vote.**

Name _____

State Your Answer – Chapter Ten
(xx points)

1. Access http://www.findlaw.com and review California Code of Civil Procedure § 1859. What does it provide regarding how statutes are to be interpreted?

    In the construction of a statute the intention of the Legislature, and in the construction of the instrument the intention of the parties, is to be pursued, if possible; and when a general and particular provision are inconsistent, the latter is paramount to the former. So a particular intent will control a general one that is inconsistent with it.

2. Access the GPO Access Web site and locate the *Weekly Compilation of Presidential Documents* for August 23, 2004 (volume 40, number 34). Whose death was recognized by President Bush in a statement? Where did the individual work during World War II?

    The President recognized the death of Julia Child who worked in the Office of Strategic Services in World War II.

3. Review the Web site of the Internal Revenue Service. Who is the current Commissioner of the IRS and where did he receive his bachelor's degree?

    The current Commissioner is Mark W. Everson who received his B.A. in history from Yale University.

4. Review title 314 of the State of Washington Administrative Code at http://www.leg.wa.gov/wac. What is the definition of "liquor"?

    "Liquor" means beer, wine, or spirits.

5. Review the Web site for the United Nations.

    a. When was the Czech Republic admitted as a member state or nation?

    The Czech Republic was admitted on January 19, 1993.

    b. How are peacekeepers compensated?

    Peacekeeping soldiers are paid by their own Governments according to their own national rank and salary scale. Countries volunteering uniformed personnel to peacekeeping operations are reimbursed by the UN at a flat rate of a little over $1,000 per soldier per month. The UN also reimburses countries for equipment.

6. Access the site for the Municipal Code Corporation (http://www.municiode.com). What does Chapter 606 (specifically section 606-3) of the Cincinnati Code of Ordinances require?

> **It shall be the duty of every person who owns or harbors a dog or dogs in the city of Cincinnati to have such dog or dogs inoculated by a veterinarian with chick-embryo rabies vaccine, and shall each three years thereafter, have the dog revaccinated with chick-embryo rabies vaccine; provided, however, that dogs shall not be required to be vaccinated before reaching the age of five months.**

7. Access the site http:///www.uscourts.gov and locate the rules for the First Circuit. What does Local Rule 32(a) require?

> **If a party is represented by counsel, one copy of its brief, petition for rehearing and all other papers exceeding ten pages in length must be submitted on a computer readable disk submitted at the time the party's paper filing is made. The brief on disk must be accompanied by nine paper copies of the brief.**

Name _____

Assignment for Chapter Eleven

(xx points)

PART I: **LEXIS**

1. Select "Get a Document" and "Get by Citation." Retrieve the case located at 534 U.S. 316.

    a. What is the LEXIS citation?   **2002 LEXIS 488**

    b. How many pages are in the case? **11**

    c. Select and click on the yellow triangle shown for this case. What does the yellow triangle mean? How many times has the case been distinguished by later cases? **The icon means "Caution – the case has possible negative treatment. As of Feb. 22, 2005, the case had been distinguished 11 times.**

    d. Which 2004 case from the First Circuit Court of Appeals cited this case?

    McGuire v. Reilly, **386 F.3d 45, 62**

2. Select "Search" at the top of the toolbar and then select the topic "Trademarks." Select "Federal and State Trademark Cases." Using natural language, locate cases relating to scandalous trademarks.

    a. Retrieve the 1993 case with the docket number 93-1464. What is the case name? *In re Mavety Media Group*

    b. Select and click on the yellow triangle shown for this case. Is there any subsequent appellate history for this case? **No**

3. Select "Get a Document" and "Get by Citation." Enter the citation 519 U.S. 2.

    a. What is the name of this case? *California v. Roy*

    b. Select "More Like This" and then "Search." What is the first case you are directed to? *United States v. Vazquez,* **271 F.3d 93**

    c. Return to your original case at 519 U.S. 2. Select "Shepardize."

244

(i) List the four categories of citing references that Shepard's indicates. **"Cautionary analyses"; "positive analyses"; "neutral analyses"; and "other sources"**

(ii) Locate the 2001 law review article that mentions the case located at 519 U.S. 2. Where is the case mentioned in this law review article? **The case is mentioned in footnote 41.**

4. Select "Get a Document" and "Get by Citation." Enter 18 U.S.C.S. § 509.

    a. What does this statute relate to, generally? **Counterfeiting and forgery**

    b. What Am. Jur. 2d reference are you directed to? **20 Am. Jur. 2d *Counterfeiting* §§ 1 et seq.**

    c. Retrieve this Am. Jur. 2d reference. What Sixth Circuit case are you directed to for the definition of "counterfeiting"? ***Richland Trust Co. v. Federal Insurance Co.*, 494 F.2d 641**

5. Select "Search" on the toolbar. Select "California" within "States Legal – US" and then select "Deerings California Codes Annotated." In the search box, use natural language and locate the Business and Professions Code statute relating to what paralegals' business cards should include.

    a. Give the citation for this statute. **Cal. Bus. & Prof. § 6452**

    b. When was this statute added? **2000**

6. Select "Get a Document" and then "Party Name" and locate a United States Supreme Court case in which the plaintiff's name is A. Elliott Archer.

    a. What is the citation for this case? **538 U.S. 314, 123 S. Ct. 1462, 155 L. Ed. 2d 454**

    b. What is the LEXIS citation for this case? **2003 U.S. LEXIS 2498**

    c. What was the disposition of this case? **Reversed and remanded**

7. Select "Search Advisor" on the toolbar. Explore the legal topic of "Cyberlaw." Explore "Defamation." What three legal topics are listed? **Damages, Defamatory Statements Online, and Internet Service Provider Liability**

8. Select "Shepard's" on the toolbar. Using the KWIC format, Shepardize 105 N.E.2d 685.

    a. What is the name of the case you are Shepardizing? ***Arthur Murray Dance Studios, Inc. v. Witter***

    b. What kind of treatment does Shepard's indicate for this case by the use of its icon? **Positive treatment**

9. Select "Get a Document" and then "Docket Number." Locate the case from the United States Court of Appeals with the docket number 73-1050.

    a. What Seventh Circuit case are you directed to? ***Popeil Bros., Inc. v. Schick Electric, Inc.*, 494 F.2d 162 (7th Cir. 1974)**

    b. Retrieve this case and then Shepardize it. What A.L.R. Fed. annotation are you directed to? **70 A.L.R. Fed. 796**

    c. Who wrote the A.L.R. Fed. annotation? **Wesley Kobylak, J.D.**

10. Select "Search" from the toolbar and then "Secondary Legal" and then "Law Reviews & Journals." Use natural language and locate U.S. articles relating to the Sarbanes-Oxley Act of 2002.

    a. What 2003 Albany Law Review article are you directed to? **67 Alb. L. Rev. 211**

    b. Review this law review article. Whom does footnote 2 quote? **Homer Simpson**

11. Select "Search" and then "Find a Source." Locate the source titled "A Dictionary of Modern Legal Usage." What is a "put" in securities law? **A put is an option to sell securities.**

246

12. Select "Search Advisor" and then "Family Law." Select "Child Custody" and then "Awards." Locate Connecticut family law cases relating to this topic. Give a brief overview of the 2005 Connecticut case in which the plaintiff's name is Denardo. **Termination of grandparents' visitation was affirmed because they failed to allege or prove their relationship with a child was similar to a parent-child relationship and denial of visitation would case real, significant harm to child.**

13. Select "Get a Document" and "Get by Citation." Retrieve Wash. Rev. Code § 26.10.160.

    a. What does this statute deal with, generally? **Nonparental actions for child custody**

    b. Shepardize this statute. What treatment was this statute given by the United States Supreme Court? **The statute was held unconstitutional in part by *Troxel v. Granville*, 530 U.S. 57, 147 L. Ed. 2d 49, 120 S. Ct. 2054.**

14. Select "Search" and then "Secondary Legal" and "Restatements." Select the Restatement (Second) of Contracts (case citations). Using natural language (and date restrictions to locate cases after January 1, 2000), locate the case discussing the prison mailbox rule.

    a. What is the name of the case? ***Huizar v. Carey***

    b. According to this case, when is a prisoner's petition deemed filed? **It is deemed filed when the prisoner hands it over to prison officials for mailing.**

    c. Review Restatement (Second) of Contracts § 63. What is the title of this Restatement provision? **"Time when acceptance takes effect."**

PART II. WESTLAW

1. At the initial Westlaw screen, in the "Find this document by citation" box, enter 568 N.W.2d 585.

    a. What is the name of this case? ***Jeffrey Lake Development, Inc. v. Central Nebraska Public Power & Irrigation District***

    b. How many pages is the case? **Approximately 14**

    c. Select "West Reporter Image." What is the first word on page 588? **"terminate"**

    d. Return to the case in its original format. What A.L.R. reference are you directed to? **15 A.L.R.3d 899**

    e. On the left side of the screen, select "KeyCite" and KeyCite this case. How many documents are listed (including this case)? **4**

    f. Give the citation for the history of this case, namely, the appeal after remand. **262 Neb. 515, 633 N.W.2d 102**

2. Select "Directory" from the toolbar and select "Directories, Reference." Select *Black's Law Dictionary* (8th ed. 2004) and locate the definition for "mistrial." What is another term for mistrial? **"abortive trial"**

3. Select "Directory" and continue selecting the appropriate databases to search Colorado cases. Use natural language and develop a query to locate cases from Colorado dealing with the liability of ski resorts for skiing injuries.

    a. What 1994 Colorado case are you directed to? ***Graven v. Vail Associates, Inc.*, 888 P.2d 310 (Colo. Ct. App. 1994)**

    b. Retrieve this case. On the left side of the screen, select "Table of Authorities." How many cases are cited in the 1994 Colorado case? **18**

    c. Return to the case. On the left side of the screen, select "Am. Jur. Proof of Facts." What section in this article discusses the rescue duty of ski patrol? **§ 20**

    d. Return to the case. What KeyCite icon is displayed? **A red flag**

e. KeyCite this case. What is the subsequent history of this case? **The judgment was reversed by** *Graven v. Vail Associates Inc.*, **909 P.2d 514 (Colo. 1995)**

4. Select the appropriate databases for federal statutes. Using natural language, locate the federal statute relating to copyright rights of attribution.

 a. What is the first statute you are directed to? **17 U.S.C.A. § 106A**

 b. Select this statute. Give the citation to the 1996 law review article by Geri J. Yonover that comments on the statute. *Precarious Balance: Moral Rights, Parody, and Fair* **Use, 14 Cardozo Arts & Ent. L. J. 79 (1996)**

 c. Select this law review article.

 (i) How many pages is this law review article? **44**

 (ii) What does Section IA of the article discuss? **"The European Experience"**

5. Select "Directory" and the appropriate databases to use the U.S.C.A. Popular Name Index.

 a. Give the citation for the "Blue Star Mothers of America Act." **36 U.S.C.A. §§ 30501-30514**

 b. Review the Act. May a corporation contribute to a political party? What section within the Act governs your answer? **No, per § 30508(b)**

6. Select "Find" on the toolbar and enter the citation 350 F.3d 810.

 a. What is the name of the case? ***Smith v. Basin Park Hotel, Inc.***

 b. Review headnote 3 and select or click on the KeyCite icon. What message is displayed? **"There are currently no KeyCite notes referenced for your headnote." [Note: This message was displayed as of 2/23/05.]**

c. Return to the case located at 350 F.3d 810. At the left of the screen, select "Petitions, Briefs, and Filings." Review the appellee's brief.

   (i) What does the Corporate Disclosure Statement state? **"Basin Park Hotel, Inc. certifies it has no parent corporation, nor does any publicly held corporation own any of its stock."**

   (ii) Review the Table of Authorities in the brief. Select the *Anderson* case. Select or click on this case. What KeyCite icon is displayed? **A yellow flag is displayed.**

   (iii) Select the KeyCite icon. What case declined to follow *Anderson*? ***Bartlett v. Mirabel*, 128 N.M. 830, 999 P.2d 1062 (2000)**

   (iv) How many green stars are displayed? **4**

   (v) Review the KeyCite box at the left of the screen. What summary is provided for you relating to the current status of this case as good law? **"Some negative history but not overruled."**

7. Select "Find" and locate the case published at 898 S.W.2d 30. Select or click on the first name identified with a blue hyperlink. Identify this individual and give his or her phone number. **Honorable Chris Piazza, Circuit Judge. Telephone number: (501) 340-8424**

8. Select "Directory" and select "Administrative Material" within the "U.S. State Materials" database. Locate the attorney general opinions for California. Using natural language, search for opinions relating to smoking bans in public places.

   a. Select the opinion from October 1999. What was the question addressed to the attorney general? **May the owner of a bar or tavern with a total of five or fewer employees permit smoking in the bar or tavern?"**

   b. What answer was provided by the attorney general? **The owner may not permit smoking.**

   c. What California statute was construed in the opinion? **Cal. Lab. Code § 6405.5**

9. Select "Directory" and "Litigation." Select "Jury Verdicts, Settlements, & Judgments" and then "Andrews Minnesota Jury Verdicts." Using natural language, retrieve information relating to medical malpractice cases decided after January 1, 2000. Select the August 2004 case relating to a teenager's death from meningitis. What was the settlement breakdown? **$94, 394.49 was paid to the parents of the decedent; $5,000 was paid to the minor brother of the decedent; and $75,605.51 was paid to the law firm for attorneys' fees and costs."**

10. Select "KeyCite" from the toolbar and KeyCite the case located at 537 U.S. 79. Review the negative indirect history. Why didn't *Scott v. First Union Securities* follow the case located at 537 U.S. 79? **"Not followed as dicta."**

11. Select "Directory" from the toolbar and then "A.L.R." Using natural language, locate annotations relating to liability for injuries to trespassers. Select the annotation published in 70 A.L.R.3d.

    a. What Idaho case is discussed in this annotation? ***O'Guin v. Bingham County*, 72 P.3d 849**

    b. Review § 2 of the annotation. What is the discernable trend in this area of law? **"The discernable trend is toward extending the scope of the landowner's liability, even in jurisdictions which continue to recognize the validity of the traditional 'status' distinctions between invitees, licensees, and trespassers. Thus, in many jurisdictions, where the presence of a trespasser is known to a landowner, or should have been anticipated by him, the duty owed is one of reasonable care under the circumstances."**

12. Select "Find" from the toolbar and then select "Find by party name." Locate a federal case in which one of the party's names is "Grokster." When did the U.S. Supreme Court grant certiorari for this case? **December 10, 2004**

13. Select "Find" from the toolbar and then select "Find this document by citation." Locate 42 U.S.C. § 1201. What does this statute relate to, generally? **Grants to states for aid to the blind**

14. Select "KeySearch" from the toolbar. Select "Corporations" and then "Piercing the Corporate Veil." Select Florida federal and state cases (with West headnotes) and "Search."

   a. What November 2003 case are you directed to? *U-Can-II v. Setzer*, **870 So. 2d 99, 28 Fla. L. Weekly 2732 (2003)**

   b. What key numbers appear in the yellow bands? **101k1.7 and 101k1.4**

   c. Review the November 2003 case and KeyCite it. What occurred on January 14, 2004? **A rehearing was denied.**

15. Select "Find" and then select "Find this document by citation" to locate the case published at 660 So. 2d 1165. Select "C" at the top of the screen. Give the name of the 1999 Florida case you are directed to. *Nextel Argentina, A.R.L. v. Elemar Intern. Forwarding, Inc. S.R.L.*

16. Select "Find" and then "Find a case by party name." How many federal cases are there in which a party's name is "Grainer"? **Three [as of 2/23/05]**

17. Select "Directory" and then A.L.R. Using natural language, locate an annotation in A.L.R.4th that relates to inhalation of asbestos (and product liability).

   a. Give the citation to the annotation. **39 A.L.R.4th 395**

   b. Who is the author of the annotation? **William B. Johnson, J.D.**

   c. What section of the annotation discusses sophisticated users of asbestos products? **Section 8b**

18. Select "Find" and then select "Find this document by citation" to locate the document designated as 2003 WL 23004289. What is this document? **This is the appellant's brief and argument in** *Herrin v. United States.*

Name _____

State Your Answer – Chapter Eleven
(xx points)

1. Access LEXIS's Directory of Online Sources at http://web.nexis.com/sources. Use the field titled "Geography" and select your state. Determine LEXIS's coverage for your state's attorney general opinions.

    Answers will vary. For California, Florida, and Texas, the coverage is January 1977 through the current time. For New York, the coverage is from February 1976 through the current time.

2. Access Westlaw's Database Directory at http://directory.westlaw.com/?tf=90&tc=11.

    a. Give the appropriate database identifier for cases from your state's courts.

    Answers will vary, but most appear to comprise the state's two-letter postal code abbreviation together with the letters "CS," as in CA-CS, FL-CS, NY-CS, and TX-CS.

    b. Give the appropriate database identifier for annotated statutes from your state.

    Answers will vary, but most appear to comprise the state's two-letter postal code abbreviation together with "ST-ANN," as in CA-ST-ANN, FL-ST-ANN, NY-ST-ANN, and TX-ST-ANN.

    c. Give the appropriate database identifier for the George Mason Law Review.
    The database identifier is GMLR.

Name _____

Assignment for Chapter Twelve
(xx points)

1. Access THOMAS.

    a. Select "Public Laws" and select for the 108th Congress. What is the purpose of P.L. 108-126? **To authorize the design and construction of a visitor center for the Vietnam Veterans Memorial.**

    b. Review the text of this law. When was it approved? **Nov. 17, 2003**

2. Return to THOMAS and locate information relating to the House Agriculture Committee.

    a. When was the committee created? **May 3, 1820**

    b. How many subcommittees does the Committee include? **Five**

3. Return to THOMAS and access the Senate Directory. Obtain information relating to Senator DeWine from Ohio.

    a. When was Senator DeWine born? **January 5, 1947**

    b. How many children does Senator DeWine have? **Eight**

    c. When was Senator DeWine first elected to the Senate? **1995**

4. Return to THOMAS and select "Historical Documents."

    a. Select the Declaration of Independence. When was it drafted? **It was drafted between June 11 and June 28, 1776.**

    b. Select the Federalist Papers. Who is the author of the General Introduction? **Hamilton** Who is the author of the 41st paper relating to powers conferred by the Constitution? **Madison**

5. Access the FirstGov site and select "A-Z Agency Index." Select the American Battle Monument Commission and review information relating to the cemetery in Normandy, France. How many graves of American military dead are in the cemetery? **9,387**

6. Return to the A-Z Agency Index for FirstGov. Select the Patent and Trademark Office.

    a. Select "Trademarks" and conduct a "basic user search" to locate the trademark "You Deserve a Break Today." When was this mark registered? **It was registered on November 20, 1973.**

    b. Select "Patents" and search for the following patent: No. 6,004,596. What is the invention patented? **It is a "sealed crustless sandwich" (essentially, it is a crustless peanut butte and jelly sandwich).**

    c. For the above patent, select "Images." What is shown on the screen? **A drawing of the round, crustless sandwich is shown.**

7. Access the site MegaLaw and select "Entertainment law." Select ASCAP and then select "ACE Title Search." By selecting "writer," locate the songs written by Billy Joel.

    a. How many songs are identified? **122**

    b. Select "Shameless." Who are identified as performers of the song? **Billy Joel and Garth Brooks**

8. Access the site www.uscourts.gov and select information relating to the U.S. Bankruptcy Courts. Review "Bankruptcy Basics." What is a Chapter 7 bankruptcy?

    It is a liquidation or straight bankruptcy, used primarily by individuals to free themselves of debt simply and inexpensively, but it may also be used by businesses that wish to liquidate.

9. Return to www.uscourts.gov and identify the address of the U.S. District Court for the Western District of Texas (San Antonio division). **655 East Durango Boulevard, Room G65, San Antonio, TX 78206**

10. Access the site for the U.S. Supreme Court (www.supremecourtus.gov) and select "Public Information." Review the Chief Justice's Year-End Report on the Federal Judiciary for 2004.

   a. Review Section II. Which circuits have not had any new judgeships for twenty years? **First, Second, and Ninth**

   b. Review Section IV. Why was there an eleven per cent increase in civil filings?

   There was 16% growth in federal question filings and many cases related to financial investments. Personal injury and product liability filings more than doubled and diversity filings grew 11%

11. Access FindLaw and select for federal laws. In the appropriate search boxes, search for 35 U.S.C. § 101. What does this statute provide? **It relates to what inventions are patentable (namely those that are novel, nonobvious, and useful).**

12. Return to FindLaw and select for U.S. Supreme Court cases.

   a. In the citation search box, search for 525 U.S. 121. What is the defendant's name? **Garrison, et al.**

   b. In the party name search box, enter "Bush" and search for *Bush v. Gore*. Who delivered the opinion of the Court? Which Justices dissented?

   The opinion was a *per curiam* opinion. There were several dissents:
   - **Justice Stevens (joined by Justices Ginsburg and Breyer);**
   - **Justice Souter (with whom Justice Breyer joined and Justices Stevens and Ginsburg joined except as to Part C);**
   - **Justice Ginsburg (joined by Justices Stevens, Souter, and Breyer); and**
   - **Justice Breyer (joined by Justices Stevens and Ginsburg except as to part I A 1, and by Justice Souter who joined as to Part 1).**

13. Access the site for GPO Access. Select the *Federal Register*, and browse the table of contents for 2004. Select the *Federal Register* table of contents for Wednesday, December 29, 2004. Review the material for the Education Department.

   a. Generally, what proposed rule is set forth? **Special Education and Rehabilitative Services: Individuals with Disabilities Education Act (IDEA) - Regulations**

   b. Review the proposed rule. When must comments be received by the Department of Education on this proposed rule? **By Feb. 28, 2005.**

Name _____

State Your Answer – Chapter Twelve
(xx points)

1. Access either FindLaw or MegaLaw. How many witnesses are needed in your state when a will is executed?

    Answers will vary, but in most states, two witnesses are needed.
    California Probate Code § 6110: two witnesses
    Florida § 732.502: two witnesses
    New York Estates, Powers, and Trusts § 3.21: two witnesses
    Texas Probate Code § 59: two witnesses

2. Access the site for the National Association for Secretaries of State (http://www.nass.org). Who is the secretary of state for your state?

    California: Bruce McPherson
    Florida: Glenda E. Hood
    New York: Randy A. Daniels
    Texas: Geoffrey S. Connor

3. Access the site Hoover's, at http://www.hoovers.com. Locate information for Delta Air Lines, Inc.

    a. What is the ticker symbol for Delta? **DAL**

    b. What is the company's phone number? **(404) 715-2600**

    c. When is the company's fiscal year-end? **December**

    d. Who are the company's top competitors?

    AMR Corp., Southwest Airlines, and UAL

4. Access the site FirstGov. Select "State Government" and then "State Legislatures." Locate your state's constitution. What is the title of Article 1 of your state's constitution?

    In California and Florida, Article I is called "Declaration of Rights."
    In New York and Texas, Article I is called "Bill of Rights."

5. Access Google. Enter "rcw 4.16.005." What are you referred to? What does this section provide?

> **Use is referred to the Revised Code of Washington § 4.16.005, which relates to the commencement of actions and provides that actions can be commenced within the periods provided in this chapter after the cause of action has accrued.**

6. Use Google and locate the home page for Oklahoma Association of Wine Producers.

> **Site is located at http://web.fvdes.com/teacher_resources/Web_Eval_TL/OKWine2/okawp.html.**

   a. Who established the first successful winery in Indian Territory?
   Sequoyah

   b. What was the value of wines in 1996? **More than $300 million**

   c. Review the copyright notice at the end of the site. What message are you given?

   > **"Everything in the preceding page is complete nonsense. There is no such thing as the Oklahoma Association of Wine Producers. It is all a fake. The page was created for use in a classroom situation to illustrate the ease with which erroneous or false information may be distributed on the Internet. Do not use or cite any information contained on that page."**

Name _____

State Your Answer – Chapter Thirteen
(xx points)

1. Access the site http://www.ll.georgetown.edu/lib/guides/cost.html. What is the last tip provided to help keep research costs under control?

   The final tip is to sign off LEXIS or Westlaw if the search is not going well and get help from the library or customer service.

2. Access the "Research Steps Tutorial" at the site http://www.lawschool.cornell.edu/lawlibrary/Finding_the_Law. What is the beginning stage of legal research?

   The beginning stage of legal research is ascertaining the meaning of technical words or phrases before opening a book. One must understand the meaning of legal terms of art. Dictionaries, thesauri, and *Words and Phrases* can help.

3. Access the site http://www.lectlaw.com/study.html and review "Ten Easy Steps to Legal Research." What is the final step?

   The final step is to check for the most current information by reviewing the newest edition, the most recent supplement, or pocket parts.

Name _____

Answer Key for Exercises for Chapter Fourteen
(xx points)

GRAMMAR

SELECT THE CORRECT WORD.

1. The deposition transcript was received by Jill and **her**/she.

2. For who/**whom** did the witness testify?

3. The SEC has released **its**/it's/its' findings.

4. Jack and him/**he** attended the hearing.

5. Someone has left **his-her**/their briefcase in the courtroom.

6. The company held it's/**its** annual meeting today.

7. The subpoena must be served on Tom, James, and he/**him**.

8. The committee, together with the members, have/**has** issued the report.

9. Each of the exhibits are/**is** indexed in the closing binder.

10. Only one of the documents for the hearings have/**has** been summarized.

SPELLING

SELECT THE CORRECT SPELLING.

1.	**admissible**	admissable
2.	decedant	**decedent**
3.	dependant	**dependent**
4.	**privilege**	privelege
5.	**occasion**	occassion
6.	**organization**	organisation

261

7.	judgement	<u>judgment</u>
8.	inadvertant	<u>inadvertent</u>
9.	**<u>interrogatories</u>**	interogatories
10.	**<u>the foregoing section</u>**	the forgoing section

PUNCTUATION

CORRECTLY PUNCTUATE THE FOLLOWING SENTENCES.

1. Both judges<u>'</u> chambers were recently redecorated.

2. The motion was heard on January 3, 2005<u>,</u> and resulted in a change of venue.

3. Following are various remedies that may be granted by a court<u>:</u> compensatory damages, punitive damages<u>,</u> and equitable relief.

4. Judge Harris<u>'s</u> opinion was lengthy.

5. The transcript<u>,</u> however<u>,</u> was not included with the other documents.

6. Alice Bowen<u>,</u> the former senator, attended the meeting.

7. The jury<u>'s</u> decision was unanimous.

8. The first witness was late<u>,</u> <u>w</u>hich made the judge angry.

   [Alternatively, two sentences may be made, as follows: The first witness was late. This made the judge angry.]

9. There were two omissions in the agreement<u>:</u> <u>T</u>hey were both in paragraph two.

10. He is an extremely diligent paralegal<u>,</u> and he is always prepared to help.

262

Name _____

State Your Answer – Chapter Fourteen
(xx points)

1. Access the Web site of the U.S. Government Printing Office Style Manual.

    a. Review Rule 3 relating to capitalization and either correct the following or indicate if they are correct.

        i. I live near the lake. Its name is **L**ake Deepcreek.

        ii. I lived in the **W**est. Travel in a westerly direction.

        iii. I live in San Diego County. The **c**ounty is large.

    b. Review Rule 8 relating to punctuation and either correct the following or indicate if they are correct.

        - Your boss's memo is complete. **(correct)**

        - The men**'s** cars were parked outside.

        - Jefferson Davis**'s** home was in Richmond.

        - The trial began in June 2004. **(Omit comma after "June.")**

        - Send me the April 15, 2005**,** report.

        - She was a tense, angry witness. **(correct)**

2. Access http://www.bartleby.com and review *The Elements of Style*.

    a. Review Section II.1 and use the correct punctuation to make the following expressions possessives: the friend of Charles, the poems of Burns, and the malice of the witch.

        Charles's friend, Burns's poems, the witch's malice

    b. Review Section II.2 and punctuate the following sentence: **He opened the letter, read it, and made a note of its contents.**

Name _____

Answer Key for Exercises for Chapter Fifteen
(xx points)

PRECISION

SELECT THE CORRECT WORD IN THE FOLLOWING SENTENCES.

1. The **effect**/affect of the expert's testimony was negligible.

2. The company's principle/**principal** office is in Atlanta.

3. She agreed to the terms of the parenting agreement during our **oral**/verbal telephone conversation.

4. The settlement was entered into between/**among** all four litigants.

5. The jury found him **liable for**/guilty of malpractice.

6. All attorneys must insure/**ensure** their clients are prepared for their depositions.

7. The jury was **affected**/effected by Ms. Lane's testimony.

8. Tina prepared the only memoranda/**memorandum** this week.

9. Beside/**Besides** the bailiff, the marshal also performed security checks in the courtroom.

10. "It's the principal/**principle** of the thing," the client told her attorney.

[Note that answers may vary for the following exercises. Following are some suggested answers.]

CLARITY

REPHRASE EACH OF THE FOLLOWING TO PRODUCE A CLEARER SENTENCE.

1. The contract was signed on April 4. The parties' agreement was later amended in May.

    The contract was signed on April 4. The contract was later amended in May.

2. We are not precluded from claiming that Dr. Smith failed to adhere to a not unreasonable standard of care.

    We may claim that Dr. Smith failed to adhere to a reasonable standard of care.

3. We do not deny that scandalous trademarks are unprotectable under the U.S. Trademark Act.

    We agree/admit/acknowledge that scandalous trademarks are unprotectable under the U.S. Trademark Act.

4. The witness arrived early for her deposition. The deponent later tired in the afternoon.

    The witness arrived early for her deposition. She/the witness later tired in the afternoon.

5. We cannot fail to allege that the defendant refused to repair the leased premises.

    We must allege that the defendant refused to repair the leased premises.

6. Although the seller paid taxes on the property, the vendor failed to obtain title insurance for the parcel.

    Although the seller paid taxes on the property, the seller failed to obtain title insurance for the parcel.

7. The defendant's motorcycle collided with the pedestrian. The motor vehicle was then sold for scrap metal.

> **The defendant's motorcycle collided with the pedestrian. The motorcycle was then sold for scrap metal.**

8. We cannot forget to ensure that Ms. Smith is not unprepared for trial.

> **We must remember to ensure that Ms. Smith is prepared for trial.**

9. Mr. Phillips told Mr. Ruiz that he must attend the settlement conference.

> **Mr. Phillips told Mr. Ruiz that Mr. Phillips/Mr. Ruiz must attend the settlement conference.**

10. The bank released the financial statements on Friday. This was a violation of its obligations to maintain the records in confidence.
> **The bank released the financial statements on Friday. This release was a violation of its obligations to maintain the financial statements in confidence.**

READABILITY

REWRITE THE FOLLOWING SENTENCES TO MAKE THEM MORE READABLE BY USING THE ACTIVE VOICE.

1. A decision was announced by the Supreme Court that affected all claims brought under the new legislation.

> **The Supreme Court announced a decision that affected all claims brought under the new legislation.**

2. The election held by the corporation resulted in approval of the directors nominated by the committee.

> **The corporation's election resulted in approval of the directors that the committee nominated.**

3. An agreement to settle the case was approved by the judge.

> **The judge approved the agreement to settle the case.**

4. A confidentiality agreement was signed by all of the company's employees.

> **All of the company's employees signed a confidentiality agreement.**

5. The transcript was prepared by the court reporter after a hearing was held by the judge.
> **The court reporter prepared the transcript after the judge's hearing.**

REWRITE THE FOLLOWING SENTENCES TO MAKE THEM MORE READABLE BY USING PARALLEL STRUCTURE.

1. The critical characteristics of effective paralegals are attention to detail, organizational skills, and being flexible.

> **The critical characteristics of effective paralegals are attention to detail, organizational skills, and <u>flexibility.</u>**

2. Indexing documents and preparation of letters to clients were two of Mary's job duties.

> **Two of Mary's job duties were indexing documents and <u>preparing</u> letters to clients.**

3. The settlement agreement required the defendant to pay $50,000, sign a confidentiality agreement, and refraining from making any further statements to the media.

> **The settlement agreement required to defendant to pay $50,000. sign a confidentiality agreement, and <u>refrain</u> from making any further statements to the media.**

4. The clients were instructed to sign the promissory note, depositing the money into the escrow account, and file a copy of the deed of trust with the clerk's office.

> **The clients were instructed to sign the promissory note, <u>deposit</u> the money into the escrow account, and file a copy of the deed of trust with the clerk's office.**

5. Careful proofreading and making edits to documents is key to ensuring their accuracy.

> **Careful proofreading and <u>editing</u> documents is key to ensuring their accuracy.**

6. There are two steps to closing the file: first, returning the original documents to the client; and secondly, preparing the summary of the file contents.

> **There are two steps to closing the file: first, returning the original documents to the client; and <u>second</u>, preparing the summary of the file contents.**

REWRITE THE FOLLOWING SENTENCES TO MAKE THEM MORE READABLE BY ELIMINATING JARGON.

1. Until such time as they execute the agreement, the parties have agreed and consented to cease and desist from any and all activities related to discovery in the instant case at bar.

> **Until they sign the agreement, the parties have agreed to cease/stop all discovery activities in this case.**

2. In the event that the document evidences fraud or deceit in its inception or making, the plaintiff shall be required to apprise the defendant antecedent to commencing litigation.

> **If the document shows fraud in its making, the plaintiff must inform the defendant before commencing litigation [or filing suit].**

3. The first parcel of land is contiguous and adjacent to the second.

> **The first parcel of land is next to the second.**

4. At her deposition, the defendant will be required to elucidate her reason for failing and refusing to consummate the purchase transaction relating to the real estate in question.

> **At her deposition, the defendant must explain her reason for failing to purchase the real estate.**

5. In reference to your lease, we opine that the remainder of the rent that is due and owing must be paid to the landlord.

> **Regarding your lease, it is our opinion [or "we believe"] that the rest of the rent owed must be paid to the landlord. [It may be possible to omit the introductory phrase "Regarding your lease."]**

Name _____

State Your Answer – Chapter Fifteen
(xx points)

1. Review the handout *Writing User-Friendly Documents* at the Plain Language Web site at http://www.plainlanguage.gov. Review page 19. What is a "noun sandwich" and how can it be avoided?

    A noun sandwich consists of groups of nouns sandwiched together. They can be avoided by using more prepositions and articles to clarify the relationships among the words in the noun cluster.

2. Review the SEC's guidance document *Plain English Handbook* at http://www.sec.gov. Review Chapter 6. What are the most common writing problems that the SEC has encountered?

    The SEC has identified the following common problems: long sentences; passive voice; weak verbs; superfluous words; legal and financial jargon; numerous defined terms; abstract words; unnecessary details; and unreadable design and layout.

3. Access Purdue University's Online Writing Lab at http://owl.english.purdue.edu. Review the handout entitled "Parallel Structure."

    a. What is the third rule that the Lab recommends to avoid problems with parallel structure?

    The OWL states "Be sure to keep all the elements in a list in the same form."

    b. What proofreading strategies are recommended to avoid problems with parallel structure?

    - **Skim your paper, pausing at the words "and" and "or." Check on each side of these words to see whether the items joined are parallel. If not, make them parallel.**

    - **If you have several items in a list, put them in a column to see if they are parallel.**

    - **Listen to the sound of the items in a list or the items being compared. Do you hear the same kinds of sounds? For example, is there a series of "-ing" words beginning each item? Or do your hear a rhythm being repeated? If something is breaking that rhythm or repetition of sound, check to see if it needs to be made parallel.**

4. Access Professor Eugene Volokh's site at http://www1.law.ucla.edu/~volokh/legalese.htm. What substitutions are recommended for the following terms of legalese: "evince," "negatively affect," and "substantiate"?

- **Substitute "show" for "evince."**
- **Substitute "hurt" or "harm" or "damage" or some such phrase for "negatively affect."**
- **Substitute "prove" for "substantiate."**

5. Access the site http://www.ccc.commnet.edu/grammar and review the information on Writer's Block. What is the worst part of the writing experience for many writers?

For many writers, the worst part of the writing experience is the very beginning.

Sample Opinion Letter for Chapter Sixteen

Notes to Instructors:

- Other styles and approaches are acceptable.

- It should be easy to revise this assignment to make it specific to any state because all states have statutes requiring foreign corporations to qualify to transact business and defining what it means to "transact business." Nearly all state laws are based upon the Model Business Corporations Act.

- This assignment requires only that students access the Act. It does not require any review of cases or other authorities.

- The Act is available at http://www.abanet.org/buslaw/library/onlinepublications/mbca2002.pdf and can be found by "Googling" the term "Model Business Corporations Act." The applicable provisions of the Act are found in Chapter 15 (specifically, Sections 15.01 and 15.02).]

- For the sake of example, the following letter assumes that the corporation is a California corporation and has been providing services in Nevada without receiving authority from Nevada to operate as a foreign corporation. In Nevada, however, the penalty is not less than $500, rather than a daily penalty, which is the case in many states.

Smith & Keane, L.L.P.
123 Elm Street
City, California 92117

[Date]

Mr. Edward Davis, President
Outdoor Artists, Inc.
678 Cedar Avenue
City, CA 92110

Re: Effect of Failure to Qualify as a Foreign Corporation

Dear Mr. Davis:

Thank you for asking us to review the consequences of a corporation's acts of transacting business without receiving permission from the state in which it is engaged in business.

As we understand them, the facts are as follows: Outdoor Artists, Inc. ("OA") is a California corporation engaged in the business of providing landscape design services. For several years, OA provided services only in California. During the past year, however, OA has provided services in Nevada. Specifically, OA opened a bank account in Nevada and performed landscaping services for five clients. One client, Leo Mahony, has refused to pay for the services and OA wishes to initiate a lawsuit to recover the money owed. Another client, Jill Lopez, has sued OA, alleging that OA damaged her drainage system when it performed landscaping services for her.

As you may know, a corporation may be formed in one state and yet do business in others. In order for a corporation to transact business lawfully in a state other than its state of incorporation it must receive permission from the second state, in which it is referred to as a "foreign" corporation. You have informed us that OA did not qualify to transact business in Nevada.

We have researched the applicable law and have concluded that although opening a bank account in Nevada did not require OA to qualify as a foreign corporation in Nevada, the acts of providing landscape services to clients in Nevada was transacting business within the meaning of the statutes.

The applicable statutes provide that a foreign corporation may not transact business in Nevada until it obtains a certificate of authority from the Nevada Secretary of State. Certain activities, however, do not constitute "transacting business." Specifically, maintaining a bank account is not considered transacting business. However, engaging in repeated transactions of a like nature, such as the landscaping services OA provided to five Nevada clients, is transacting business, and OA should have applied for and received a certificate of authority from the Nevada Secretary of State before it engaged in those activities.

There are several consequences of transacting business without authority. First, OA may not maintain any lawsuit in Nevada until it obtains a certificate of authority. Thus, OA cannot initiate litigation against Leo Mahony at this time. However, OA may continue to defend itself in the action brought by Jill Lopez. Finally, OA is liable for a civil penalty of $ ___ for each day (but not to exceed $____ for each year) it transacts business in Nevada without a certificate of authority.

To minimize the monetary penalty, we advise that OA immediately cease conducting any business in Nevada and apply to the Nevada Secretary of State for a certificate of authority to transact business in Nevada. The process is fairly straightforward and can likely be accomplished within a matter of days. As soon as OA has received its certificate of authority, it may initiate litigation against Leo Mahony to recover the money owed by him to OA.

We suggest that after you have had an opportunity to review this letter, that you contact us to discuss this matter further and provide us with your instruction to obtain the certificate of authority from the Nevada Secretary of State. Because the monetary penalty will continue to accrue each day that OA transacts business in Nevada without authority, it is critical that action be taken immediately.

Please feel free to contact us if you have any questions or comments.

Sincerely,

Alison Keane

Name _____

State Your Answer – Chapter Sixteen
(xx points)

1. Access the site http://writing.colostate.edu/references/documents/bletter/index.cfm.

    a. Review the section relating to formatting letters. How should the complementary close be punctuated?

    Only the first word in a multiple word closing should be capitalized. All phrases should be followed by commas.

    b. Review the section called "Effective Letter-Writing Principles." Why do many executives prefer written documents over other forms of communication?

    A written document may serve as a contract, it puts the facts on record, and it ensures that people aren't required to rely on memory only.

2. Access the site http://www.business-letter-writing.com. Review the checklist for writing business letters. What four tips are given?

    The four tips are to keep letters short, simple, strong, and sincere.

MEMORANDUM ASSIGNMENT – CHAPTER SEVENTEEN

Note to Instructors: There are numerous cases relating to the issues presented by the fact scenario. Thus, you may wish to restrict research efforts to authorities from your state.

Student memos should cover the three primary issues raised by the fact scenario:

- If the original support order was made expressly nonmodifiable, Tina cannot petition to modify it.

- Spousal support will be increased only upon a material change in financial circumstances and a showing that the original order was unfair and unreasonable when it was made. Moreover, the purpose of spousal support is to maintain the supported spouse in the style he or she enjoyed during the marriage. Thus, Tina cannot obtain a modification that will enable her to live at a higher scale than she enjoyed while married.

- Orders relating to child support and custody are always reviewable. The standard for modifying child support is not as stringent as that for modifying spousal support. Some courts have held that an increase in the supporting parent's financial condition alone (without any showing of increased needs of the child) will justify an increase in child support.

- **Citations**: Citations are shown below in *Bluebook* format. The format for *ALWD* is identical except as follows:

    o Use "Cal. App. 1st Dist." rather than "Cal. Ct. App." for the *Smith* and *Catalano* cases;

    o Use "Colo. App." rather than "Colo. Ct. App." for the *Aldinger* and *Caufman* cases;

    o Use "Ill. App. 1st Dist." rather than "Ill. App. Ct." for the *Arnold* case and "Ill. App. 2d Dist." rather than "Ill. App. Ct." for the *Boyden* case;

    o Use "Md. Spec. App." rather than "Md. Ct. Spec. App." for the *Ware* case;

    o Use "Minn. App." rather than "Minn. Ct. App." for the *Cisek* case; and

    o Use "Wis. App." rather than "Wis. Ct. App." for the *Gerrits* case.

MEMORANDUM

To: Attorney

From: Paralegal

Re: Modification of Spousal Support

Date: Month Day, Year

FACTS

Two years ago, our client, Tina Wolf, was divorced from her husband of twelve years, Tom, a successful investment banker. As part of the divorce judgment (which incorporated Tina and Tom's voluntarily agreed upon divorce settlement agreement), Tina was awarded monthly spousal support. This spousal support has been sufficient to meet Tina's needs. The couple's two children reside with Tina, and Tom pays monthly child support, which is also adequate to meet the children's needs. Last month, Tom won the lottery in our state. Tom will now receive approximately $700,000 per year from the state lottery for the next thirty years. Tina would like to know if she can seek a modification of her spousal support and receive increased spousal support based on Tom's significant change in circumstances.

ISSUE

May a court modify an order of spousal support based on the paying spouse's improvement in financial condition due to lottery winnings?

BRIEF ANSWER

Unless a divorce order is expressly nonmodifiable, a court may modify support obligations, but only if there is a material increase in the supporting spouse's ability to pay, the original order was unfair and unreasonable, and as a result of the modification the supported spouse will not be living at a standard higher than that enjoyed during the marriage.

DISCUSSION

1. Modification of Spousal Support Agreements

While many courts have held that lottery prizes won during a marriage or before a judgment of divorce are generally marital property subject to distribution in divorce proceedings, *e.g., Lynch v. Lynch*, 791 P.2d 653 (Ariz. 1990) and *Ware v. Ware*, 748 A.2d 1031, 1034 (Md. Ct. Spec. App. 2000), respectively, once a judgment of divorce has been entered, the issue is more complicated.

The threshold question that must be answered is whether the spousal support obligations (also called "alimony" and "maintenance," depending upon the jurisdiction) are fixed or final. In *Day v. Day*, 717 A.2d 914, 916 (Me. 1998), a divorced couple's separation agreement was incorporated into the court's divorce judgment. The agreement provided that the ex-husband's alimony obligations were fixed and final and would not be subject to modification of any kind. When the ex-wife later won a state lottery, the ex-husband petitioned the court to reduce his alimony obligations. The court held that while generally a court may modify an award of alimony upon a showing of a substantial change in either party's financial condition, in that case, the award could not be modified because by its terms (which were incorporated into the court's final divorce judgment), it was nonmodifiable.

Generally, parties may fashion private settlement agreements, and divorce courts will incorporate these provisions into the final divorce decree. These separation agreements may expressly prohibit modification of terms set forth in a divorce decree relating to spousal support; however, terms concerning support, custody, and visitation of children are always subject to modification. *Aldinger v. Aldinger*, 813 P.2d 836, 839 (Colo. Ct. App. 1991). Nevertheless, provisions restricting the jurisdiction of the court to modify maintenance are strictly construed, and only when parties expressly agree to preclude modification are spousal support obligations incapable of modification. *Sinn v. Sinn*, 696 P.2d 333, 336 (Colo. 1985). Moreover, if there is silence on the issue and the trial court makes no provision to review maintenance, maintenance may later be modified (assuming there is a showing of substantial and changed circumstances). *In re Caufman*, 829 P.2d 501, 502 (Colo. Ct. App. 1992).

Thus, in the present case, it must first be determined whether the couple's settlement agreement, which was incorporated into the divorce decree, included specific provisions prohibiting later modification of its terms relating to spousal support. Unless the agreement expressly and unequivocally prohibits such modification, its terms relating to spousal support may be modified (assuming all other conditions relating to modification exist).

2. **Standard for Modification of Spousal Support Provisions**

Unless an agreement as to spousal support is final and fixed, generally, a court may modify an award of spousal support upon a showing of a substantial change in either party's financial condition. *Haag v. Haag*, 609 A.2d 1164, 1165 (Me. 1992). Lottery proceeds won after a divorce may be considered a change in financial circumstances in determining whether a modification of maintenance is justified. *Gerrits v. Gerrits*, 482 N.W.2d 134, 137 (Wis. Ct. App. 1992).

However, in evaluating whether to modify spousal support, courts take into account not only the supporting spouse's ability to pay an increased amount but also the needs of the supported spouse. *E.g., In re Marriage of Smith*, 274 Cal. Rptr. 911, 918 (Cal Ct. App. 1990). Thus, a number of courts have held that a party wishing to modify an award of spousal support must first prove that the existing order, when made, was insufficient to meet his or her reasonable needs or that the reasonable costs of satisfying those needs has increased. After such a showing, the moving party must then prove the supporting spouse's ability to pay increased support. *Id.* at 917.

Some courts have gone further and stated that not only must a spouse seeking modification of a support award show a substantial change in circumstances, but also must show that the change has the effect of rendering the original award of spousal support unreasonable and unfair. *Beck v. Kaplan*, 566 N.W.2d 723, 726 (Minn. 1997). In *Caufman,* 829 P.2d at 502, the court went further and stated that if a trial court makes no provision to review maintenance, maintenance may be modified only upon a showing of changed circumstances so substantial and continuing as to make the original award "unconscionable."

In *Cisek v. Cisek*, 409 N.W.2d 233, 236 (Minn. Ct. App. 1987), after a divorce, and after the parties stipulated to the amount of maintenance to be paid to the ex-wife, the ex- husband's income increased by four hundred percent. The court rejected the ex-wife's request for modification of maintenance, holding that a favorable change in an ex-spouse's income, absent a showing that maintenance is unfair and unreasonable, does not constitute sufficient grounds to change a stipulated financial arrangement incorporated into a divorce decree. Thus, because Tina and Tom agreed to the support to be paid to

Tina, and this agreement was incorporated into the divorce decree, and because Tina has acknowledged that the amount she currently receives has been and is adequate to meet her needs, unless she can show both a substantial increase in Tom's financial situation and that the existing obligation is unfair, the support arrangement will not be modified.

In *Gerrits*, 482 N.W.2d at 138, five months after a divorce judgment ending a 42-year marriage became final, the ex-husband won $19 million in a state lottery. The ex-wife petitioned for an increase in spousal support or maintenance based on the former husband's substantial change in financial condition. The court thoroughly examined the purpose of maintenance and stated that the underlying purpose of maintenance (either when it is initially ordered or later modified) is to maintain the payee spouse at the financial level or standard of living enjoyed during the marriage. *Id.* In *Gerrits*, the appellate court reversed a judgment ordering an increase in the ex-wife's maintenance on the basis that the trial court did not determine what amount would be reasonably needed to maintain the standard of living she enjoyed during her marriage. Moreover, the court cautioned that it is only the rare couple that can maintain a predivorce living standard after parting. *Id.* In fact, because the purpose of "maintenance" is, in fact, to *maintain*, the recipient is generally not entitled to live at a scale higher than that the recipient enjoyed while married. *E.g, Arnold v. Arnold*, 76 N.E.2d 335, 338 (Ill. App. Ct. 1947).

In the present case, the amount awarded to Tina is admittedly sufficient to satisfy her needs. It must be determined whether the amount awarded is sufficient to maintain the standard of living Tina enjoyed during the marriage (although, as the court noted in *Gerrits*, 482 N.W.2d at 138, both parties must bear sacrifices that the cost of an additional household imposes). If the amount currently paid to Tina is insufficient to maintain a standard of living comparable to what she enjoyed during the marriage, or if Tina can show that the original award was unfair and unreasonable when it was made, she may be able to secure an increase in her spousal support. Because it may be difficult in the extreme for Tina to prove either of these conditions, it seems unlikely that Tina would prevail in any attempt to obtain an upward increase in her spousal support.

3.   Modification of Child Support Provisions

Although Tina may fail in her attempt to modify the spousal support award, she should consider seeking an increase in Tom's child support obligations. The rule that an increase in spousal support must be based upon some relationship to the standard of living of the parties during marriage is inapplicable to modifications of *child* support. *In re Marriage of Catalano*, 251 Cal. Rptr. 370, 375 (Cal. Ct. App. 1988). As noted earlier, even if Tina and Tom have expressly agreed to preclude modification of spousal support, such an agreement is inapplicable to child support, *Aldinger*, 813 P.2d at 830, and Tina may seek an increase in child support payments.

In *In re Marriage of Boyden*, 517 N.E.2d 1144, 1146 (Ill. App. Ct. 1987), a father's obligations to pay child support were suspended when the father became unemployed. When the father later won a substantial lottery prize, the mother sought to modify the child support award. The court stated that the fact that the child had grown older and the costs of living had risen were proper bases for establishing an increased need. The court further noted that a court may order child support in excess of the known needs of the child; the court can consider the standard of living the child would have enjoyed had the marriage not been dissolved and the financial resources of the noncustodial parent. *Id.* In fact, a modification of child support is *required* when there is a substantial imbalance between the supporting parents' capabilities and a child's needs. *Boyden*, 517 N.E.2d at 1146.

Some courts have held that an increase in a noncustodial parent's ability to pay can, by itself, provide a proper basis for an increase in child support, without any proven increase in needs of the children. *E.g., Graham v. Graham*, 597 A.2d 355, 356 (D.C. Ct. App. 1991).

Further, in *In re Marriage of Bussey*, 483 N.E.2d 1229, 1234 (Ill. 1985), the court stated that a child is not expected to live at a minimal level of comfort while the noncustodial parent is living a life of luxury. "Accordingly, where the supporting parent enjoys a lifestyle that far exceeds that of the custodial parent, child support must to some degree reflect the more opulent lifestyle *even though this may, as a practical matter, produce a benefit for the custodial parent.*" *Catalano*, 251 Cal. Rptr. at 376 (emphasis added).

Thus, even without a showing by Tina of increased needs of her children (which may be easily met as they grow older), a substantial imbalance between Tom's capabilities and the children's needs may support an increase in child support, even though Tina may incidentally benefit from this increase as well.

CONCLUSION

Unless Tina and Tom expressly agreed that provisions of their settlement agreement relating to support of Tina would not be modified, a court may modify a spousal support award if there has been a material change of circumstances such that the original award is unfair or unreasonable. However, generally, a recipient of spousal support is entitled only to receive support in an amount necessary to maintain the standard of living enjoyed during marriage and not to live at a scale higher than the recipient had during marriage. Thus, given the fact that Tina's needs are currently being met, it will be extremely difficult for Tina to obtain an increase in spousal support based on Tom's change in financial condition. However, because the standard for modification of child support awards is different from that for spousal support awards, Tina should consider seeking an increase of child support, based upon the fact that Tom's financial situation has materially improved and the children likely have increased needs as they have grown older. Moreover, some courts have suggested than a material increase in the noncustodial parent's income alone can be a basis for increasing child support.

Name _____

State Your Answer – Chapter Seventeen
(xx points)

1. Access the site http://www.lawnerds.com/guide/irac.html.

    a. What is the key to issue spotting?

    The key to issue spotting is being able to identify which facts raise which issues.

    b. Review the section called "Conclusion." What is a common mistake made by many students in conclusions?

    Students often make the mistake of not taking a position one way or the other on an issue. Another common mistake is to conclude something without having a basis for the conclusion or opinion.

2. Access the site http://www.ccc.commnet.edu/grammar. Review the information relating to thesis statements. Give the definition of a thesis statement.

    A thesis statement is that sentence or two in your text that contains the focus of your essay and tells your reader what the essay is going to be about.

3. Access the site http://www.yourlawprof.com/21f/law34/legalmemonotes.htm. What are the three functions of a legal memorandum?

    The three functions and reasons to prepare a legal memoranda are as follows: Writers won't know research is done until they try to write it up; a memo provides an accessible record of the fruits of research; and the results of research must be communicated to another.

Sample Brief for Chapter Eighteen

Note to Instructors:

Many other styles and formats for the court brief are also acceptable. Cases cited and relied upon by students will vary; however, most of the cases cited in the following brief are well-known or landmark cases relating to prayer at school graduations and other functions. In particular, the *Lee v. Weisman* and *Santa Fe Independent School District v. Doe* cases should be thoroughly discussed. Many students will choose to examine the issue according to the three-pronged test outlined in *Lemon v. Kurtzman*, 403 U.S. 602 (1971), and, in fact, the Court in *Santa Fe* used the *Lemon* test in its analysis. In addition, an excellent A.L.R. Fed. annotation thoroughly examines the issues raised by the fact pattern. *See* Deborah Sprenger, Annotation, *Giving of Invocation with Religious Content at Public School-Sponsored Events to Which the Public is Invited or Admitted as Violation of Establishment Clause of First Amendment*, 98 A.L.R. Fed. 203.

Citations given are in *Bluebook* and *ALWD* form. Note that according to *ALWD*, parallel citations may be given for U.S. Supreme Court cases and that consecutive pages may be shown, for example, as *id.* at 165-66 or *id.* at 165-66.

IN THE UNITED STATES DISTRICT COURT

FOR THE ANYWHERE DISTRICT

Marisa Bailey,   )

    Plaintiff   )

    v.   )   No. 05-0118

Rio Grande Unified School District,)

    Defendant   )

_____)

MOTION FOR SUMMARY JUDGMENT

Pursuant to Fed. R. Civ. P. 56(c), Defendant Rio Grand Unified School District (the "District") respectfully requests that this Court grant its Motion for Summary Judgment.

STATEMENT OF FACTS

This action, brought by Plaintiff Marisa Bailey ("Bailey") against the District, arises out of the following factual situation. All facts are undisputed.

Bailey is an 18-year old high school senior who attends James River High School ("James River"). James River is operated by Rio Grande Unified School District (the "District"), a school district that operates elementary, middle, and secondary schools in the Anywhere District. In planning its graduation ceremony and program, James River notified parents of the graduating seniors that student-led and student-initiated nondenominational prayers would be offered at the graduation. School officials at James

River will review any prayers before they are offered at the ceremony. Attendance at graduation is voluntary.

Ms. Bailey has sued the District on the basis that such prayers would violate the First Amendment's prohibition against laws relating to establishment of religion.

I.

A SCHOOL DISTRICT'S POLICY OF APPROVING PRAYERS AT A SCHOOL GRADUATION VIOLATES THE EQUAL PROTECTION CLAUSE

The First Amendment to the Constitution provides that "Congress shall make no law respecting an establishment of religion, or prohibiting the free exercise thereof." U.S. Const. amend. I. The Fourteenth Amendment imposes this prohibition on the individual states. *Wallace v. Jaffree*, 472 U.S. 38, 49-50 (1985).

The seminal case dealing with the issue of school-sponsored prayer is *Lee v. Weisman*, 505 U.S. 577 (1992), in which the U.S. Supreme Court ruled that school-sponsored prayers at graduation ceremonies violate the First Amendment to the Constitution. In *Lee*, members of the clergy were invited by a public school to give invocations and benedictions at middle and high school graduations (at which attendance was voluntary) in Providence, Rhode Island. The school issued written guidelines to the clergy members to offer nonsectarian prayers. The prayers were challenged by one of the graduates and her father as unconstitutional.

The Court first noted that although attendance at the graduation ceremonies was not required to receive a diploma, attendance and participation were "in a fair and real sense, obligatory," *id.* at 586, because "to say that a teenager has a real choice not to attend her high school graduation is formalistic in the extreme." *Id.* at 594. Thus, Bailey's attendance at the James River graduation is not voluntary but rather compulsory.

The Court then held that it was "beyond dispute that, at a minimum, the Constitution guarantees that government may not coerce anyone to support or participate in religion or its exercise, or otherwise act in a way which 'establishes a religion or religious faith, or tends to do so.' " *Id.* at 587 (quoting *Lynch v. Donnelly*, 486 U.S. 668, 678 (1984)).

In addition, although the First Amendment provides that the government may accommodate the free exercise of religion, that principle does not supersede the fundamental limitations imposed by the Establishment Clause, specifically, that the state may not compel religious observance. The Court noted the significant degree of control exercised by the state (namely, the school district) at its graduation by dictating the contents of the program, the speeches, the timing, and the dress and decorum of the students. The Court held that prayers by clergy selected by the school combined with this control to make the prayer a "state-sanctioned religious exercise in which the student was left with no alternative but to submit." *Id.* at 597. This coercive element together with compulsory attendance at the ceremony combined to produce a violation of the Establishment Clause.

Likewise, in the present case, although the District does not require Bailey to attend graduation to obtain her diploma, the District's control over the ceremony and the normal teenage desire to attend one's graduation place public and peer pressure on Bailey to attend the ceremony. As in *Lee*, Bailey's attendance at the graduation is thus obligatory. Similar to the situation in *Lee*, James River exercises significant control over the ceremony in that it dictates the content of the program and reviews the prayers to be offered. These two elements (obligatory attendance and control over the ceremony) produce a coercive atmosphere and "establish" a religious practice by the state in violation of the Establishment Clause.

Moreover, the fact that the prayers offered at the ceremony are nonsectarian or nondenominational will not protect the prayers from Constitutional scrutiny. In *Lee*, the Court discussed the good faith and sectarian nature of the prayers offered and concluded as follows:

> The question is not the good faith of the school in attempting to make the prayer acceptable to most persons, but the legitimacy of its undertaking that enterprise at all when the object is to produce a prayer to be used in a formal religious exercise which students, for all practical purposes are obliged to attend.

Id. at 588-89.

The Court in *Lee* thus held that the school's policy of offering prayers at school graduations violated the First Amendment in that it compelled students to participate in a religious activity organized and controlled by the school.

In the present case, although Bailey is not required to attend graduation, there are subtle and indirect pressures that, in effect, compel her attendance at a ceremony controlled by the District. In addition, as held in *Lee*, even nondenominational or nonsectarian prayers may not be established by the government at school graduation ceremonies. Thus, the nondenominational types of prayers to be offered at the James River graduation violate the Establishment Clause.

II.

A STUDENT-LED INVOCATION AT HIGH SCHOOL EVENTS CONTROLLED BY A SCHOOL VIOLATES THE ESTABLISHMENT CLAUSE

Although it is clear after *Lee* that clergy-led prayers at high school graduation ceremonies are unconstitutional, a variation on that issue is presented by this case: student-led prayers. In *Santa Fe Independent School District v. Doe*, 530 U.S. 290 (2000), the Court was called upon to determine the constitutionality of a school's practice of allowing student-led and student-initiated "messages," "statements," or "invocations" over the public address system before football games if students had voted to include these messages at the games and then voted to select a speaker. The school contended that the messages offered by the students were private student speech and not public or governmental speech that endorsed religion and that the election system ensured constitutionality. The Court concluded, however, that fundamental Constitutional rights may not be submitted to a vote. The Constitution requires that minority views be treated with the same respect as those of the majority. The student referendum in *Santa Fe* did nothing to protect the rights of the minority; in fact, it placed the students with dissenting views at the mercy of the majority.

The Court held that the school district in *Santa Fe* had failed to divorce itself from the religious elements present in the invocations. Although the district had attempted to distance itself from the religious messages by initiating the student referendum process, the elections took place only because the school had chosen to permit the students to deliver the invocation. *Id.* at 306. Likewise, the school's policy required that the message "solemnize the event" and consist of an "invocation," a word that traditionally describes a religious message. *Id.* at 306-07. Finally, the school sponsored the football games on its property and broadcast the message over its public address system. In such a context, the members of the listening audience must perceive the pregame prayer as stamped with the school's "seal of approval." *Id.* at 308-09. The Court acknowledged that although attendance at the extracurricular football games was not required, there was likely sufficient peer pressure on students to attend the games and that some students such as members of the team, band, and cheerleaders, were in fact required to attend the games. The delivery of a pregame prayer would coerce those present to participate in an act of religious worship. *Id.* at 312.

As applied to the present case, *Santa Fe* clearly shows that student-led invocations offered pursuant to a school policy are not private speech but are rather school-sponsored prayer in view of the fact that they are authorized and regulated by the District's policy and take place on school property at a school-related event.

III.

A SCHOOL-APPROVED INVOCATION IS A RELIGIOUS MESSAGE AND VIOLATES THE ESTABLISHMENT CLAUSE

Although the District may argue that *Adler v. Duval County School District*, 250 F.3d 1330 (11th Cir. 2001) permits prayer at high school graduations, the facts in *Adler* are significantly different from those in the present case. In *Adler*, students voted on whether to permit a student message at the beginning or closing of the graduation ceremony and, if so, which student was to deliver the message. The student selected had the option of deciding not to deliver any message. The school had no authority to review or monitor the message if one was to be given.

In determining that the facts were distinguishable from those in *Santa Fe*, the court in *Adler* noted that the school did not select the messenger, the school did not select the content of any message, and the student could select whether there would be any message at all. In contrast, in *Santa Fe*, the speech was state-sponsored rather than private because the speech was subject to regulations that confined the content and topic of the message and the school district's policy, by its very terms, invited and encouraged religious messages. The court in *Adler* held that the ability to regulate the content of speech is a hallmark of state involvement. *Id.* at 1337. Although it was possible that the student might choose on his or her own to deliver a religious message, that result was not preordained. The decision whether to give a message and the content of the message was the uncensored and wholly unreviewable decision of the student speaker. Thus, the speech in *Adler* was private speech and not state-sponsored endorsement of a religious event.

In the present case, James River has determined that an invocation will be delivered at its graduation, and the school has the ability to review the content of the invocation message. These facts place this case squarely in line with *Lee* and *Santa Fe* and serve to distinguish it entirely from *Adler*. The regulation of the graduation ceremony and of the content of the invocation show state involvement by the District and accordingly, a violation of the Establishment Clause.

IV.

THE DISTRICT'S PRACTICE VIOLATES THE *LEMON* TEST IN THAT THE INVOCATION IS RELIGIOUS AND IT ADVANCES RELIGION

To determine whether a certain act or practice violates the Establishment Clause, courts rely on the three-pronged test developed in *Lemon v. Kurtzman*, 403 U.S. 602, 612 (1971), in which the Court held that to be valid under the Establishment Clause, an act must have a secular purpose, its primary effect must not either advance or inhibit religion, and it cannot create an excessive entanglement of the government with religion. If the action violates any of these three prongs or tests, then it must be invalidated. *Stone v. Graham*, 449 U.S. 39, 40-41 (1980).

In *Adler*, 250 F.3d at 1334, the court reviewed the *Lemon* test and concluded that the defendant school district's policy met all three prongs of the test: The policy had a secular purpose by affording graduating students an opportunity to direct their own graduating ceremony and permitting student freedom of expression; the text of the policy did not disclose a religious purpose; and there was no excessive entanglement between the school and religious figures because any message would be student-led.

In contrast, in the present case, the District's policy fails the *Lemon* test. As held in Santa *Fe*, 530 U.S. at 306, an "invocation" is a term that primarily describes an appeal for religious assistance. It is an "undeniable truth" that prayer is inherently religious. *Graham v. Central Community School District*, 608 F. Supp. 531, 535 (S.D. Iowa 1985). Thus, the purpose of the invocation to be offered at the James River graduation is not a secular purpose but is rather a religious one. Second, as the court noted in *Graham*, 608

F. Supp. at 536, "a prayer, because it is religious, does advance religion." Thus, the District's acts violate the second prong of the *Lemon* test. The third prong of the *Lemon* test need not be examined because the District's acts clearly fail the first two prongs of *Lemon*, and, if government action violates any of the three *Lemon* tests, it violates the Establishment Clause. *Stone*, 449 U.S. at 40-41 (1980).

CONCLUSION

For the foregoing reasons, this Court is respectfully urged to grant Bailey's Motion for Summary Judgment.

                                                                           Respectfully submitted,

Date: _____   _____

Assignment for Chapter 18
(xx points)

[Note to Instructors: Because neither the *Bluebook* nor *ALWD* provide rules for citations in tables of authorities, answers may vary. For example, some individuals may prefer to abbreviate words in citations as if they were in "stand alone" format, while others may prefer to present citations in more complete form, as if they were in "textual sentence" format.]

Table of Authorities (*Bluebook* format)

Cases

Daly v. O'Brien, 109 F.3d 111 (8th Cir. 2000)
DeLansing v. Kirk, 525 U.S. 909 (2002)
Forrest v. Sullivan Insurance Indemnity Co., 520 U.S. 16 (2001)
Gregory v. Young, 121 F.3d 889 (8th Cir. 2002)
In re Walsh, 799 N.E.2d 52 (N.Y. 1991)
Lehman v. Moore, 909 F.2d 550 (3d Cir. 1998)
Nelson v. Lyons, 15 F. Supp. 3d (D.N.J. 2001)
State v. Reynolds, 789 N.E.2d 199 (N.Y. 1989)

Statutes

15 U.S.C. § 1051(a) (2000)
15 U.S.C. § 1051(b) (2000)
42 U.S.C. § 2242 (2000)

N.Y. Com. Law § 330 (McKinney Year)
N.Y. Dom. Rel. Law § 445 (McKinney Year)

Table of Authorities (*ALWD* format)

<u>Cases</u>

Daly v. O'Brien, 109 F.3d 111 (8th Cir. 2000)
DeLansing v. Kirk, 525 U.S. 909 (2002) [Note: *ALWD* Rule 12.4(b) permits
 parallel citations for U.S. Supreme Court cases to be included.]

Forrest v. Sullivan Insurance Indemnity Co., 520 U.S. 16 (2001) [See note above.]
Gregory v. Young, 121 F.3d 889 (8th Cir. 2002)
In re Walsh, 799 N.E.2d 52 (N.Y. 1991) [Note: *ALWD* omits parallel citations.]
Lehman v. Moore, 909 F.2d 550 (3d Cir. 1998)
Nelson v. Lyons, 15 F. Supp. 3d (D.N.J. 2001)
State v. Reynolds, 789 N.E.2d 199 (N.Y. 1989) [Note: *ALWD* omits parallel citations.]

<u>Statutes</u>

15 U.S.C. § 1051(a) (2000)
15 U.S.C. § 1051(b) (2000)
42 U.S.C. § 2242 (2000)

N.Y. Commerce Law § 330 (McKinney Year) [Note: *ALWD* App. 3 shows no
 Abbreviation for "Commerce."]
N.Y. Dom. Rel. Law § 445 (McKinney Year)

Name _____

State Your Answer – Chapter Eighteen
(xx points)

1. Use MegaLaw (http://www.megalaw.com) to access the local rules for the First Circuit Court of Appeals. Review Rule 32. What is the maximum length for a reply brief?

    The maximum length for a reply brief is 15 pages. [Answer is found at http://www.ca1.uscourts.gov/rules/rulespg.htm.]

2. Access the site http://www.ualr.edu/~cmbarger. Select "Appellate Resources" and then "Persuasive Strategies for Appellate Brief-Writing." What is the first strategy?

    The first strategy is "You cannot convince another unless you first convince yourself."

3. Access the site http://www.appellate.net/briefs. Review the amicus curiae brief filed in *Anderson v. General Motors Corp*. What is the argument heading for Argument I?

    THE COMPENSATORY AWARDS ARE GROSSLY EXCESSIVE AND SHOULD BE SET ASIDE.

4. Access MegaLaw. What cases can be found for your state?

    Answers will vary.

California:	**Supreme Court and Court of Appeals cases from 1934 to present**
Florida:	**Supreme Court cases from September 1995 to present.**
New York:	**Court of Appeals cases from 1990 to present.**
Texas:	**Supreme Court and Court of Appeals slip opinions from 1997 to present**

Name _____

Assignment for Chapter Nineteen
(xx points)

[**Note to instructors:** Spellings or typos are corrected showing **boldface type**, omissions are shown <u>underscored</u>, and additions are shown in *italics*.]

Our client, Jack Patterson, is a convicted sex **offender** who was convicted of incest. Patterson **pleaded** guilty and was given a **ten-year** sentence to be followed by three years<u>_</u> of supervised probation. As part of <u>his</u> *Patterson's* **sentence**, the court barred Patterson from using a computer or any other device with Internet capabilities, even in the performance of his job. The judge who imposed the sentence stated that the risk of **Patterson** reoffending <u>is</u> *was* **too** great to allow him to have any Internet access. The court noted that **Patterson** could use the **Internet** [note: "Internet" should consistently appear as either "Internet" or "internet"] to lure young victims and engage in **pornography**.

There have been a number of cases in this circuit and other **circuits that** have discussed this issue. Most of those cases have held that restrictions on computer and **Internet** use are overly **broad** and are **unreasonable** if they are not related to the **convict's** crime. In the **present** case, Patterson did not use the Internet to engage in the criminal act of incest. **It's** been held that it makes no more sense to deny an offender Internet access than to bar a wire fraud perpetrator access to <u>their</u> *a [or "his or her"]* telephone.

Patterson's **background is** in information technology**,** and to provide for himself he will need Internet access upon his release from prison. Patterson has asked us to research the following <u>two</u> *three* issues: *Does a court* <u>do they</u> have the right to bar him from using the Internet, may the bar be **permanent**, and whether *is* the sentence is reasonably related to his crime.

Please prepare a written **memorandum** for **me** by Friday morning. a.m.

Name _____

State Your Answer – Chapter Nineteen
(xx points)

1. Access the site http://www.ucc.vt.edu/stdysk/proofing.html.

   a. Why does it help to read aloud?

   Reading aloud forces the reader to slow down. Additionally, it allows one to hear what is read as well as to see it, so that two senses are used.

   b. How many times do professional editors proofread a document?

   They may proofread a document as many as ten times.

2. Review the Federal Rule of Appellate Procedure 32 for the Ninth Circuit at http://www.ca9.uscourts.gov.

   a. What type styles may be used in documents?

   Fed. R. App. P. 32(a)(6) states that the document must be set in a plain roman style, although italics or boldface may be used as emphasis.

   b. What word counts are imposed for principal briefs?

   Fed. R. App. P. 32(a)(7)(B) states that a principal brief is acceptable if in contains not more than 14,000 words (or if it uses monospaced typeface and includes not more than 1,300 lines of text).

3. Review the proofreading marks found at http://www.prenhall.com/author_guide/proofing.html.

   a. What does the mark "flush" mean?

   It means "no indentation."

   b. What does the mark "Eq #" mean?

   It means to equalize the space between words.

TEST BANK

The following is a concise Test Bank, providing true-false, fill-in-the-blank, and short answer questions. Not all chapters are covered in the Test Bank, and it is intended to offer some questions instructors may use for quizzes or to develop their own examinations.

Test Questions for Chapters One and Two

1. The doctrine of *stare decisis* protects litigants from unfair and unpredictable results in cases. **T**

2. Administrative agencies such as the FDA have no power to affect your daily life. **F**

3. Dictum in a case is persuasive only. **T**

4. A court that has jurisdiction over a case automatically has venue in the case. **F**

5. A court with limited jurisdiction may hear only a certain type of case, for example, a probate case. **T**

6. A constitution is a primary source. **T**

7. In a criminal action, the injured party is the plaintiff in the case. **F**

8. A case from Kansas is binding in Ohio. **F**

9. The jurisdiction of the federal courts extends to every type of case and controversy. **F**

10. Generally, litigants are entitled to one appeal as a matter of right. **T**

11. Once an appellate court finds any error in a trial court's handling of a case, it will reverse the trial court judgment. **F**

12. Some states have such low population that they have no federal district courts. **F**

13. Each of the intermediate federal circuit courts of appeal is free to make its own decisions independently of what the other circuits have held. **T**

14. If necessary, Congress has the authority to create additional district courts and additional intermediate courts of appeal. **T**

15. The U.S. Supreme Court works on a "seniority system" such that once the Chief Justice resigns, the next most senior Justice becomes the Chief Justice. **F**

16. All federal judges are appointed by the president. **T**

17. The United States Supreme Court may act as a trial court.   T

18. Litigants have an automatic right to a grant of their petitions for writs of *certiorari*.   F

19. Cases from the state courts may be appealed to the U.S. Supreme Court if a federal question exists and *certiorari* is granted.   T

20. All states have a two-tier appellate system (meaning there are two chances for appeal after a trial).   F

21. All state court judges are elected.   F

22. A depository library is open to members of the public.   T

23. Distinguish between common law and civil law.
    Common law focuses on following similar cases as precedents because this is an equitable way of treating people who are similarly situated. Civil law countries follow comprehensive codes and place much heavier reliance on their statutes than on their case law.

24. Identify the sources of law in the United States.
    In the United States, law comes from cases, constitutions, statutes, administrative regulations and decisions, and from certain influences exerted by the executive branch relating to its policies on enforcing laws (and from treaties made by the executive branch).

25. Why are federal agencies often considered to play a unique role in our legal system?
    Federal agencies function both quasi-legislatively and quasi-judicially. In contrast to the three main branches of government, which each performs one function, the agencies perform two functions: they act like a legislature by promulgating rules and regulations; and they act like a judiciary by hearing disputes and rendering decisions.

26. The power or authority to hear a case is referred to as ___**jurisdiction**___.

27. Distinguish between the holding in a case and dictum.
    The holding in a case is authoritative and must be followed in later, Relevant cases. Dictum in a case is persuasive only.

28. Fully describe the types of cases that federal courts may hear (i.e., describe the jurisdiction of our federal courts).

> **Federal courts have <u>federal question or subject matter jurisdiction</u> and may hear any cases involving federal questions (that is, cases arising under the U.S. Constitution or any U.S. law). Federal courts also have <u>diversity jurisdiction</u> and may hear cases in which the plaintiffs have diverse residencies or domiciles, such that no plaintiff is from the same state as any defendant (and assuming that the amount in controversy exceeds $75,000).**

29. The amount in controversy in diversity cases is __**in excess of $75,000**__.

30. If a case may be brought in more than one court, jurisdiction is said to be __**concurrent**__.

31. What does it mean to say that there is no one legal system in the United States?

> **In the United States there is a legal system for the federal government (and there are federal statutes and cases) and one for each of the states (each of which has its own statutes and cases). In addition the District of Columbia has its own statutes and cases. Therefore, there are really fifty-two legal systems in the United States.**

32. Describe the basic structure of the federal court system.

> **The federal court system comprises district courts (the trial courts in the system, at least one of which is in each state), thirteen intermediate circuit courts of appeal that hear appeals from district court cases, and the U.S. Supreme Court, which has original jurisdiction in a few matters and appellate jurisdiction in others.**

33. Dawn, a resident of Wyoming, is furious with various residential and commercial developments occurring on the edge of federal parkland in Colorado. May Dawn bring an action in federal court? Discuss.

> **No. Dawn does not have <u>standing</u> to sue. She must personally suffer some actual or threatened legal injury. She cannot base her claim on the rights or interests of other people. The standing requirement ensures that the parties before a court have a personal stake in the outcome of the controversy.**

34. Frank's petition for *certiorari* to the U.S. Supreme Court was just denied. Does this mean that the Supreme Court agrees with the reasoning of the court below? Discuss.

> **No. Denial of *certiorari* is not an endorsement of the lower court action. It means simply that for reasons of judicial economy, not every case can be heard. Frank had a trial and an appeal, and this should be sufficient to satisfy the cause of justice.**

35. What factors might cause the U.S. Supreme Court to grant *certiorari* in a case?

There are no clearly articulated or published criteria followed by the Court in granting cert. The guideline most frequently given is that *certiorari* will be granted if there are "compelling" reasons for doing so. Generally, however, if the lower courts are in conflict on a certain issue and contradictory opinions are being issued, the Court might grant cert so it can resolve the conflict. Similarly, if a case is of general importance, the Court may grant cert.

Test Questions for Chapters Three through Twelve

1. Nearly all courts give great weight to legislative history. — F

2. Because of its chronological arrangement, the set *U.S. Statutes at Large* is an easy set for researchers to use to find federal laws. — F

3. The term "official" when used in connection with the publication of legal authorities means that the set of books should always be favored over an unofficial set. — F

4. For most purposes, the sets U.S.C.A. and U.S.C.S. are equivalent. — T

5. If a book has been published within the last two years, there is no need to check its pocket part. — F

6. The organization, publication, and process of finding state statutes is nearly identical to that for federal statutes. — T

7. If you violate a rule or regulation of a federal agency such as the FTC, you can be punished. — T

8. All cases decided by courts are published. — F

9. An "official" set of case reporters is of better quality than its "unofficial" counterpart. — F

10. For citation purposes, the date a case is decided is more important than the date the case was argued. — T

11. Because they are so carefully prepared by publishers such as West, you may rely upon and quote from case headnotes. — F

12. Many state cases have two and sometimes even three citations. — T

13. All states publish their cases both officially and unofficially. — F

14. Cases from our lower federal courts are not published officially. — T

15. West created the American Digest System by authority of the federal government and thus West's 400 topics of the law have governmental approval. — F

16. Many secondary authorities are highly respected and credible. — T

17.	Researchers who need a basic and general introduction to an area of law often consult a legal encyclopedia.	T
18.	The encyclopedia C.J.S. is much more highly regarded than its competitor set Am. Jur. 2d.	F
19.	Because legal periodicals are the products of law schools and their student editors, they are considered weak and elementary sources.	F
20.	A treatise is always a one-volume text.	F
21.	Many experts consider the Restatements to be the most highly regarded of all secondary authorities.	T
22.	The process of legal research requires legal researchers to follow a rigid and specified series of steps in order to find the "right" answer.	F
23.	Newer cases are always better than older cases.	F
24.	Researchers must always Shepardize or KeyCite their primary authorities, even if the authorities are one day old.	T
25.	Computer-assisted legal research is always more effective than conventional legal research (using print publications).	F
26.	LEXIS and Westlaw are roughly equivalent systems.	T
27.	Conducting legal research on the Internet will provide as thorough results as conducting legal research in a well-stocked law library.	F
28.	It is easier to get distracted when researching using the Internet than when researching conventional print volumes.	T
29.	A.L.R. annotations are primary sources.	F
30.	Because cases can be complicated, researchers often need to read a case several times to understand it.	T
31.	Because there are so many published cases in the United States, it is highly likely that you will find a published case identical to the one you are researching.	F
32.	Opinions of the United States Attorney General are binding, primary authorities.	F

33. There is no one perfect form for a case brief. **T**

34. A case brief should include the author's personal opinions regarding the import and effect of the case. **F**

35. The most important part of a case brief is the reasoning. **T**

36. Explain the difference between primary and secondary authorities.
    Primary authorities are the law themselves – the official pronouncements of the law by one of the three branches of government and thus they are binding authorities (assuming they are relevant). Secondary authorities discuss and explain the primary authorities and help one locate primary authorities. They are not binding upon a court or other tribunal but are persuasive only.

37. Classify the following authorities as either primary or secondary:

The case *Plessy v. Ferguson*	**Primary**
The Restatement (Second) of Torts § 13	**Secondary**
17 U.S.C. § 109 (2000)	**Primary**
14 Am. Jur. 2d *Contracts* § 43 (1986)	**Secondary**
45 A.L.R.3d 119	**Secondary**
A book written by Chief Justice Rehnquist	**Secondary**
An FDA regulation	**Primary**

38. What does the term "annotated" mean with reference to statutes, such as U.S.C.A. or U.S.C.S.?
    "Annotated" means "with notes" and refers to the fact that after the statutory language is given, readers will be given short notes referring them to cases interpreting the statute.

39. What are the two functions of a pocket part for a set such as U.S.C.A. or U.S.C.S.?
    Pocket parts tell researchers whether the statute they are reading is still "good law" (whether it has been amended, repealed, and so forth) and whether there are newer cases interpreting the statute (issued after the date the hardbound volume was published).

40. What advantage does an annotated set of statutes afford over an unannotated set such as U.S.C.?
    An annotated set provides not only the language of the statutes, but through the use of short annotations or notes (one sentence summaries), directs users to cases interpreting and construing the statute. An unannotated set provides merely the language of the statute. Thus, an annotated set affords more complete research

because under our concept of stare decisis, it is not the naked language of a statute that controls but rather how a court interprets that statute.

41. Describe the three research techniques used to find statutes.
Descriptive word/fact approach: This technique requires users to think of words or phrases describing a research problem and then look those up in alphabetically arranged indexes. The index will then direct the user to the appropriate statute.
Title/Topic approach: If a researcher is sufficiently familiar with the way statutes are arranged, a researcher might bypass the general index and go directly to the appropriate title and start browsing the statutes. This technique works best for those who are familiar with certain topics and titles.
Popular name approach: Because some statutes are known by their popular names, a researcher can look these up by examining the alphabetically arranged tables of statutes by popular name.

42. Our federal administrative regulations are initially published in the **Federal Register** and are then codified in the **Code of Federal Regulations**.

43. Two citations that refer to the same case are called **parallel citations**.

44. The soft-cover sets of books in which cases are initially published and which are later replaced by hardbound sets are called **advance sheets**.

45. What does a case name such as *In re Smith* indicate?
It indicates that the case is a nonadversarial matter, such as a bankruptcy or probate matter.

46. What is the advantage of reading the case summary or case synopsis and the headnotes before reading a case in full?
The case summary provides a quick overview about the case so that readers can quickly determine whether the case is relevant to the issue they are researching. If so, they can read the case in full. If not, they won't waste precious time reading a case that will not be helpful. The headnotes provide the same function and also locate the specific place in a case where a topic is discussed.

47. An opinion of the whole court in which no specific author is identified is called a **per curiam** opinion.

48. What advantage is there to a law firm in Georgia that purchases the *Southeastern Reporter* rather than the *Georgia Reports*?
The *Southeastern Reporter* will provide not only Georgia cases but will also provide cases from North Carolina, South Carolina, Virginia,

and West Virginia. Thus, the user will have access to cases from neighboring states in the event there is no case on point in his or her jurisdiction (here, Georgia).

49. What is the primary function of a digest?
Digests serve as case finders. They help researchers find numerous cases dealing with the same point of law.

50. When might a researcher use the *American Digest System* rather than the *California Digest*?
The *American Digest System* is most useful when researchers need cases from throughout the United States, perhaps for a comprehensive research project.

51. When might you consider starting your research efforts using *C.J.S.* or *Am. Jur. 2d* rather than with the annotated statutes or digests?
Encyclopedias are particularly useful for providing elementary discussions of areas of law. Thus, for researchers unfamiliar with an area of law, starting with an encyclopedia helps researchers "get their feet wet" before examining other, often more complex, authorities.

52. The periodical publications of law schools are usually called __**law reviews**__.

53. You have been asked to draft a fairly basic lease. What should you do?
After reviewing the file and after determining if the office has any form leases that would be of help, a researcher should use a <u>formbook</u> to help draft this document. Formbooks provide excellent advice, tips, and suggested language for drafting forms.

54. Mary needs to locate an attorney in Cleveland to assist on a patent case that her Boston law firm is handling. How can Mary go about locating the right attorney?
Mary should consult *Martindale-Hubbell Law Directory*, which is a directory of attorneys. The Directory provides biographical information about attorneys, allowing Mary to find an attorney experienced in the area of patent law.

55. The two primary guides to citation form in the United States are __**the *Bluebook* and *ALWD***__.

56. The method researchers use to determine if the primary authorities they rely on are still good law is called __**Shepardizing or KeyCiting**__.

57. What are some of the advantages of validating cases electronically rather than in the print volumes of *Shepard's Citations*?
Electronic validation is quicker, easier, and more current than using the print volumes. Additionally, results are provided in plain English

rather than through the use of some of the quirky abbreviations that are used in the print volumes of *Shepard's Citations*.

58. What are the two primary reasons researchers must validate the primary authorities on which they rely?

    Validation (such as Shepardizing) will not only tell researchers whether the cases and other primary authorities that they rely on are still good law, it will direct researchers to other sources that may be of valuable research assistance.

59. What is "Boolean" searching?

    Boolean searching uses symbols, numbers, and connectors when searching computers. These symbols, etc. help overcome the literalness of the computer and locate pertinent results.

60. When might it be best to start your research efforts using LEXIS or Westlaw?

    Computer-assisted legal research is extremely useful when a researcher already knows the citation to a case or other authority; when looking for cases involving a known party or attorney; when the area of law is new or evolving; when looking for the most current information available; and when validating authorities by either Shepardizing or KeyCiting.

61. List three "cautions" to exercise or be aware of when conducting legal research on the Internet.
    - **It's easy to become distracted and jump from site to site.**
    - **Reading on the screen causes eyestrain.**
    - **Projects conducted solely on the Internet lack depth and critical analysis.**
    - **Researchers may "lose" a valuable site and become disconnected from valuable information if they fail to take notes.**
    - **There are gaps in information on the Internet.**
    - **Much of the material on the Internet is anonymous and may not be reliable.**
    - **It is often difficult to determine how current information posted on the Internet may be.**

62. Another name for a treaty is __**convention**__.

63. The best-known legal directory in the United States is __***Martindale-Hubbell Law Directory***__.

64. The term used to describe the background and documents underlying an enacted statute is __**legislative history**__.

65. When might a researcher choose to make an argument based on the legislative history of a statute?
> **If it is difficult to determine the meaning of a statute, a researcher may elect to argue that its meaning can be determined by its legislative history. This may occur if the statute is so new that there are few, if any, cases interpreting it (or perhaps the cases that interpret it are contrary to the position the researcher is arguing).**

66. A case that is factually similar and legally relevant from a court in your jurisdiction that is equivalent to or higher than the court hearing your case is often called a **case on all fours or a case on point**.

67. The technique of case analysis in which researchers find similarities in cases and then compare them is called **analogy**.

68. How might a researcher handle cases that are adverse to the position the researcher is arguing?
> **A researcher will attempt to distinguish cases that are adverse to the client's position. The researcher will point out as many differences as possible to show that the adverse case(s) cannot or should not govern his or her present case.**

69. What is the IRAC method of analyzing cases?
> **Under the IRAC method, writers present the Issue, then the Rule or legal authority that governs the issue, then the writer Analyzes or Applies the rule to the writer's particular case situation, and finally, presents a Conclusion.**

70. What does it mean to say that an issue or fact is "relevant"?
> **A relevant issue or fact is one that contributes to a court's decision. Had the fact or issue been different, the ultimate decision in the case would have been different as well.**

71. A short, written summary and analysis of a published case is called a **case brief**.

72. The actual disposition of a case is called **the holding**.

73. Distinguish among majority, dissenting, and concurring opinions.
> **A majority opinion is the law. It is written by a justice in the majority. A dissenting opinion is one in disagreement with the majority opinion. A concurring opinion is one written by a justice who agrees with the result reached in a case but disagrees with the reasoning relied upon. Only the majority opinion is binding law.**

74. Written opinions by the nation's chief executive officer or a state's chief executive officer are called __**attorneys general opinions**__.

75. What is the advantage of looseleaf services?
    Looseleaf services are generally used for areas of law that involve frequent change. The sets are kept very current through the use of replacement pages that are inserted into these ringed binders or looseleaf sets. Thus, the sets afford current information without requiring an entire set to be replaced. Moreover, looseleaf sets are a type of mini-law library in that they usually afford complete coverage of a topic (for example, securities law).

76. Why is it important for an internal office memorandum to be neutral?
    An internal office memorandum is not discoverable; thus, it can set forth both the good and the bad about a case with no fear of the adverse party discovering a case's weak points. It should be neutral and objective so that everyone in an office will understand both the strong and weak points about a case so that the client can be better represented. It is better to understand the weak point about a case rather than to be "blindsided" later on.

77. The two national or general encyclopedias are __**C.J.S. and Am. Jur. 2d.**__.

78. The American Digest System is often called the __**Decennial Digest System**__.

79. Why are readers prohibited from quoting from a case synopsis or syllabus?
    The case synopsis or syllabus gives a good snapshot or idea what the case is about, but it is written by the publisher of the case reports and not by the court. Thus, it is an editorial enhancement provided by the publisher to help researchers, and it is not part of the case.

80. What is the function of "star paging"?
    Star paging tells a reader who is using an unofficial case reporter what page he or she would be looking at if the reader were viewing an official set. Citation rules for the *Bluebook* require citation to the official *United States Reports*; star paging allows consumers to purchase unofficial sets (such as L. Ed. 2d and S. Ct.) and yet cite to the *United States Reports*.

81. At his criminal trial, John was found guilty of breaking and entering into Tom's home. May the appellate court set aside this finding? Discuss.
    No. Appellate courts assume that facts found at a trial are true (unless they are totally unsupported by the record). The appellate

court cannot substitute its judgment for that of the jury or judge and determine that John did not break and enter into Tom's house.

82. Why do appellate courts give great deference to the conduct of a trial by a trial court?

Appellate courts understand that the trial court was in the best position to evaluate the credibility of witnesses and make various "on the spot" determinations. Only if the trial court clearly erred or abused its discretion will its decisions be reversed.

Test Questions for Chapters Fifteen through Nineteen

1. Generally, only paralegals engaged in litigation need good writing skills. — F

2. The more jargon used by legal professionals, the more a writing is likely to impress clients because it will sound like it has been written by a skilled lawyer. — F

3. So long as a roughly equivalent word is selected for a certain word in a written communication, the document will be acceptable and accurate. — F

4. Using vague and nondescriptive words such as "situation" and "issue" is a good way to deflect attention from a weak argument. — F

5. A good writing style is one that is invisible because it is poor writing that is noticeable. — T

6. The more complicated that a topic is, the more important is the need for readability. — T

7. The passive voice is stronger and generally shorter than the active voice. — F

8. Using "made up" words such as "liaising" adds interest and drama to a written document. — F

9. Generally, longer legal documents are of higher quality than shorter ones because the author has taken the time and effort to explain complicated legal concepts. — F

10. All letters should include a "re" line. — T

11. Paralegals often sign legal opinion letters. — F

12. Email tends to be more conversational than traditional paper communication. — T

13. Using humor in email is an effective icebreaker because humor is so easily understood in written communications. — F

14. In a letter, it is acceptable to threaten criminal prosecution if the reader will not comply with a valid demand. — F

15. In a legal memorandum, the goal is to argue the law convincingly. — F

16. In a court brief, even the table of contents and headings provide opportunities to be persuasive.   T

17. Failure to comply with a court rule establishing the maximum number of pages in a trial brief can cause a brief to be rejected by the court.   T

18. Filing an answer to a complaint is easily accomplished because most of the work is simply filling in the blanks on pre-printed forms provided by the court.   F

19. Writers should always begin with page one, section one of a writing and proceed logically and sequentially to the conclusion.   F

20. Most writers think that proofreading and reviewing are the easiest of all writing tasks.   F

21. Most law firms and offices use standard proofreaders' marks to show changes to documents.   T

22. Understanding the basics of writing (grammar, punctuation, and spelling) is not important because it is the message or content of a legal writing that is critical.   F

23. Legal writers can always avoid jargon or "legalese."   F

24. The current movement in legal writing is toward __**plain English**__ so that readers will be able to comprehend documents quickly and easily.

25. List at least three guidelines for writing in plain English (note that the SEC identifies eight guidelines).
    - **Use short sentences**
    - **Use definite, concrete, everyday language**
    - **Use active voice**
    - **Use tables and lists to present complex information**
    - **Avoid legal and financial jargon and highly technical information**
    - **Avoid multiple negatives**
    - **Avoid weak verbs, abstract terms, and superfluous words**
    - **Enhance readability through attractive design and layout**

26. The most important characteristic of legal writing is __**accuracy**__.

27. Referring to a person as "intractable" rather than "firm" is an error in __**word connotation (or possibly jargon)**__.

28. Throughout a document, Stacy has referred to one of the parties as the "Licensor." On page 10, Stacy begins referring to this party as the "Franchisor." What type of writing error is this and what is its effect?

    Switching terms such as this is "elegant variation" and readers may well think that in addition to the Licensor, there is another party to the document, namely, the Franchisor. Readers will assume that Stacy consciously selected a different term for this different party.

29. What is the "standard" word order or common sentence structure in English? Why does this order help readers?

    The standard word order is to place the subject first, the verb second, and the object third. This order helps readers because most readers expect sentences to be phrased this way, it forces sentences to be written in the active voice, and because readers typically need a subject and a verb to make sense of a sentence, this order helps readers grasp the meaning of the sentence quickly.

30. Why do writing experts always advocate writing in the active rather than the passive voice?

    - **The active voice focuses attention on the subject of the sentence that performs or causes action.**
    - **The active voice is consistent with the standard sentence structure of subject, verb, and object.**
    - **The active voice is stronger and more forceful than the passive voice.**
    - **The active voice often produces shorter sentences.**

31. How do lists enhance readability?

    Lists help readers comprehend information quickly. Rather than wading through a long narrative discussion, readers can easily identify the components of the list. Lists also create visual interest because they are set apart from the rest of the text.

32. When a writer takes a verb such as "state" and turns it into the phrase "make a statement," the writer has used a ___**nominalization**___.

33. Identify the two most critical parts of a sentence, namely, the two components readers need to make sense of a sentence.

    Readers need a subject and a verb to make sense of a sentence.

34. Why do large gaps and numerous words placed between subjects and verbs impair readability?

    Because readers need a subject and a verb to make sense of a sentence, if there is a large gap between these two components, readers can no longer remember what the sentence is about by the time they locate the verb.

35. Identify the three types of legal correspondence.
    - **General correspondence**
    - **Demand letters**
    - **Opinion letters**

36. Why should you send a confirming letter to an adversary to confirm the date that a responsive pleading is due when the adversary grants an extension of time?
    A confirming letter will ensure that there is no dispute as to when the pleading is due. Confirming letters also keep the file in order and show the progress of a case. Finally, a confirming letter provides a way of thanking the other party who provided the extension.

37. Why should a writer include a statement of facts in an opinion letter?
    The facts should be included because even a minor factual error can cause an incorrect opinion. Include the facts so the reader understands that the accuracy of the opinion depends upon the specific facts recited.

38. Why is it a good idea to call a party before sending a facsimile communication to the party?
    The document may be confidential and the receiving party may wish to pick it up in person, especially if the facsimile machine is in an open location or is shared with others.

39. The phrase "to quickly run" is an example of a __**split infinitive**__.

40. Why is it possible for legal memoranda prepared by your office to be objective and identify client's case's weaknesses?
    The memo is an internal document and is prepared for use within the firm or office. It is generally protected by the work product privilege and won't be discoverable. Because it is not discoverable, it can be objective. Also, the office or firm needs to know both the "good and the bad" about its case.

41. The principal characteristic of an office memorandum is __**objectivity**__.

42. Identify the elements of an office memorandum.
    - **Introductory information (person for whom it is prepared, person who prepared it, the subject matter, and date of preparation)**
    - **Question(s) presented**
    - **Brief Answer(s)**
    - **Statement of Facts**
    - **Analysis or Discussion**
    - **Conclusion**

43. How do legal briefs differ from memoranda?

    Legal briefs differ from memoranda in their purpose and audience. While a memorandum is intended primarily to inform and explain (generally, internally within an office or firm), briefs are intended to persuade judges.

44. In the course of preparing a memorandum of law to file in a trial court, a paralegal discovers a case that is adverse to the client's position. How should this be handled?

    The paralegal should discuss this issue with the supervising attorney. There is an ethical duty to be honest and to bring to the court's attention anything that would assist the court in making its decision. This adverse case should be addressed in a straightforward fashion and then distinguished from the client's position.

45. A lease, an employment agreement, and minutes of a corporate meeting are all examples of **transactional** documents.

46. Identify some tips or strategies that can be used to break writers' block.
    - **Write something – write anything.**
    - **Begin with the section of the paper with which the writer is most comfortable.**
    - **"Tell the story" of the project to another.**
    - **Set challenges and goals for the tasks involved.**
    - **Make a list of all items that need to be done for the project and do the easiest items first.**

47. Why are writers advised to use outlines?

    Outlines organize the structure of a writing. They provide a roadmap for the writer and remind him or her of what order in which to discuss topics, how much time to devote to these topics, and so forth. Planning ahead by using an outline will save time later.

48. Why is it often a good idea to "go public" and announce a deadline to a supervisor?

    Going public by telling a supervisor when he or she will have a finished project will force a procrastinating writer to meet this deadline. Once the deadline is announced in such a public way, the writer will force himself or herself to meet this deadline.

49. Identify some techniques that make proofreading more successful.
    - **If possible, the writer should get some distance from the project, by allowing some time to elapse between writing and proofing because it is very difficult to review a project with which one is too familiar.**
    - **Read the project aloud either alone or with a partner.**

- Use a rule or piece of paper under each line as you read the document (either aloud or silently). This prevents the reader from jumping ahead.
- Read sections out of order.

50. Why should writers work on the "design" of their documents?

    Even if a project is well written, clear, and readable, it should be presented in such a manner that it creates a favorable impression on the reader. Thus, document design enhances written projects.

51. Why is the first person (*I, my, our*, and so forth) seldom used in documents other than legal correspondence?

    Generally, in most instances, the focus should be kept on the client or party on whose behalf the writing is prepared. Thus, because the writing is on behalf of the client, third person is appropriate.

52. What is the danger in using too many quotations in a project?

    Over quoting will make the writing appear as if it has been assembled from a hodgepodge of authorities rather than being the result of careful and reasoned legal analysis. Quotations cannot just be dropped into a project. Their relevance must be explained.

53. What are some cautions to be aware of in using formbooks to draft legal documents?

    Formbooks can provide great ideas for drafting documents; however, no two situations are alike and using a form without examining it thoroughly may lead to drafting errors. Over reliance on forms may cause mistakes. Thus, writers should use formbooks, but not be slavish to them.